Effective Faith

Faith that Makes a Difference

Effective Faith

Faith that Makes a Difference

Bishop Thomas J. Tobin

Seraphina Press
212 3rd Avenue North, Suite 290
Minneapolis, MN 55401
612.455.2293
www.SeraphinaPress.com

Cover design and photo by Fernando Botelho

ISBN - 978-0-9798246-9-2
ISBN - 0-9798246-9-9
LCCN - 2009933702

Book sales for North America and international:
Itasca Books, 3501 Highway 100 South, Suite 220
Minneapolis, MN 55416
Phone: 952.345.4488 (toll free 1.800.901.3480)
Fax: 952.920.0541; email to orders@itascabooks.com

Printed in the United States of America

CONTENTS

FAITH THROUGH THE SEASONS

FAITH THROUGH THE LIFE OF THE CHURCH

FOREWORD

Cardinal Seán P. O'Malley, OFM Cap.
Archbishop of Boston

If we really believe the faith we profess, sharing the Good News is not an option; it is an imperative. Jesus' words are a living testament; they should be part of our daily lives, through what we say and what we do, from the time we get up in the morning until we fall into bed at night. Our faith is a gift that we should talk about and share with the people God has placed in our paths.

For twelve years Bishop Thomas J. Tobin has generously provided an accessible and effective means of sharing the faith through his regular weekly column, *Without a Doubt*. From its inception in 1996 as a regular feature in *The Catholic Exponent*, the newspaper of the Diocese of Youngstown, Ohio, to its present place in *The Rhode Island Catholic*, the column has given readers the opportunity to share Bishop Tobin's wisdom, insights, humor and, most importantly, his deep and abiding love of God and the Roman Catholic Church.

Evangelization is the mission of the Church, which is itself an extension of Jesus Christ, the Teacher, who wants to communicate to us life in abundance. The mission of the Church is about making disciples, helping people respond to the call to holiness by being part of a faith-filled, worshipping community committed to the Gospel.

Bishop Tobin's columns help to bring the teaching of our faith to everyday life and to gain a better understanding of why the Church teaches what it does. In the midst of a world that challenges the notion of the Church as having a rightful place in the debate on social issues and public policy, it is important that we have the resources to help us understand Church teaching, especially as it applies to respecting life and family and the good of all people.

Catholics in the United States have worked arduously to pass on the faith and to educate our young people to be good citizens of this country, the world and our eternal homeland. The content of our teaching must always embrace the truth about Christ: The Son of the Father, true God and true man, our crucified redeemer, our risen Lord who has promised to be with us always and who establishes His Church on the rock of Peter. Bishop Tobin upholds these foundational truths in all cases at all times, whether addressing the lighthearted moments of our lives or the most serious and difficult experiences. His fidelity and the courage of his convictions are a gift for all of us.

A teacher of the faith must first be a disciple to Christ, and must love the Church. Bishop Tobin's life and ministry are dedicated to fulfilling these requirements with distinction. Through this collection of *Without a Doubt* columns, I invite you to join me in sharing the bishop's reflections. May these help us all to draw closer to our Lord and to fulfill our call to be His witnesses in the world.

ACKNOWLEDGEMENTS

Jesus said to them, "Amen, I say to you, if you
have faith the size of a mustard seed,
you will say to this mountain,
'Move from here to there,' and it will move.
Nothing will be impossible for you." (Mt 17:20)

My guess is that most preachers and authors of
newspaper columns don't begin their work with
a preconceived theme in mind. Rather, they preach and
write about things that are important to them, topics that
are relevant for their times, and discover only later on that
a theme has emerged from their work.

So it is with the collection of articles in this book. If
indeed any theme has emerged from my writing, it is that
faith makes a difference, that it has a profound effect in
our daily lives. If we believe in Jesus Christ, that truth is
so important that it touches every aspect of our life, every
thought and word and deed. Faith changes our perspective
of life and informs our participation in the nitty-gritty
of the world. It is the vocation of the Christian, armed
with faith, to be "the salt of the earth" and the "light of
the world." "Your light must shine before others," Jesus
instructed his disciples. (Cf. Mt 5:13-16) Faith, then, has a
proper place in the classroom and courtroom, the bedroom
and boardroom, and indeed everywhere else the Christian
appears.

It's that conviction that underlines the columns
I've written for *The Catholic Exponent* in the Diocese of
Youngstown and *The Rhode Island Catholic* in the Diocese

of Providence. I extend my sincere gratitude to the staff of those two fine papers for their professional expertise and assistance. In particular, I am grateful to Michael Guilfoyle, Director of Communications of the Diocese of Providence, for his daily support of my communication efforts and his valuable assistance in producing this little book. And without a doubt, in writing my columns, I've been encouraged by the interest and affirmation of the devoted laity of the two dioceses in which I've been privileged to serve.

I would also like to express my sincere gratitude to Cardinal Sean O'Malley, Archbishop of Boston, for his generous words contained in the foreword of *Effective Faith*. Cardinal O'Malley's service and ministry to the Catholic Church in Boston is a wonderful example of faith in action.

I dedicate this book to Monsignor John Hagerty of the Diocese of Erie, one of the great priests of our time and a dear friend; and to all the priests who throughout the years have served as my pastors and teachers, my mentors and friends. In word and example, in personal sanctity and faithful ministry, they've shown me what it means to live the faith.

Jesus said that if we had faith the size of a tiny mustard seed we could move mighty mountains. Maybe it's an exaggeration, maybe not. But I am convinced that with effective faith we can form minds, change hearts and enlighten the world in which we live. And that's even more impressive than moving mountains!

Everyday Faith

CHAPTER 1

Abortion 101

I t seems to me that public opinion polls must always be approached cautiously. So often the results are influenced by subjective factors: Exactly how were the questions phrased? Who was asking the questions? Did the pollster have a personal agenda? How were the participants in the poll selected?

By any measure, however, the results of a recent Rhode Island poll on attitudes about abortion are very discouraging. According to a *Providence Journal* report, 63 percent of Rhode Islanders identified themselves as "pro-choice." Just 32 percent identified themselves as "pro-life." And this in the state often identified as having the highest percentage of Catholics in the nation. "Judged exclusively on those numbers, Rhode Island stands well into the abortion-rights corner" concludes the newspaper article. Embarrassing, isn't it?

The results suggest that as a Catholic community in Rhode Island we need to return to some basic teachings about the evil of abortion. Political and sociological arguments aside, we need to affirm again, in the clearest possible language, that abortion is wrong, evil and sinful. Even the most difficult circumstances of a pregnancy don't alter the outcome of an abortion. When an abortion takes place, a baby dies. A Catholic doesn't have the option of being "pro-choice" if that choice leads to the death of a child.

Catholic teaching on this serious matter is very clear.

The Second Vatican Council

"God, the Lord of life, has entrusted to women and men the noble mission of safeguarding life and they must carry it out in a manner worthy of themselves. Life must be protected with the utmost care from the moment of conception: abortion and infanticide are abominable crimes." *(Gaudium et Spes, #51)*

The Catechism of the Catholic Church:

"Since the first century the Church has affirmed the moral evil of every procured abortion. This teaching has not changed and remains unchangeable. Direct abortion, that is to say, abortion willed either as an end or a means, is gravely contrary to the moral law." *(#2271)*

Pope John Paul II

"The deliberate decision to deprive an innocent human being of his life is always morally evil and can never be licit as an end in itself or as a means to a good end... Among all the crimes which can be committed against life, procured abortion has characteristics making it particularly serious and deplorable." *(Evangelium Vitae, #57-58)*

The Bishops of the United States:

"Human life is a gift from God, sacred and inviolable. Because every human person is created in the image and likeness of God, we have a duty to defend human life from conception until natural death and in every condition. . . Abortion, the deliberate killing of a human being before birth, is never morally acceptable." (*Faithful Citizenship, 2003, p. 17*)

And for those who prefer a less hierarchical, but just as compelling view on abortion, Blessed Mother Teresa of Calcutta: "Life is a gift that God has given us. That life is present even in the unborn. A human hand should never end a life. I am convinced that the screams of the children whose lives have been terminated before their birth reach God's ears."

Now, even as I write this I know some will object asking, "What about the other issues related to human life? What about war, capital punishment, violence, poverty and abuse?" Well it's certainly true that these issues are important and legitimate pro-life concerns. "War is always a defeat for humanity" said Pope John Paul. Capital punishment cannot be justified in our country, the Bishops of the U.S. have stated. And violence, poverty and abuse are terrible evils that cause untold suffering for many individuals, especially women and children, around the world, in our country and in our own local community.

But there can be legitimate debates about these issues. There is, at least in Christian theory, a "just war." Likewise, a government may impose the death penalty if certain conditions exist. And while no Christian worthy of the name can ignore the dire consequences of violence, poverty and abuse, there are various opinions about the most effective ways of responding to these issues.

Abortion is different. It is always intrinsically evil. There are no circumstances that justify abortion. Its victims are innocent and defenseless, and number in the millions. Without a doubt, abortion is the fallacious foundation upon which the culture of death builds its ugly edifice.

Being passionately committed to other human life issues does not excuse an individual from personally and publicly opposing the grave sin of abortion.

Nonetheless, I wonder if it's possible for us to reach a consensus about the pro-life agenda. What would happen if those who oppose abortion as the primary issue became more active in responding to other human life concerns? And what if those who are sincerely concerned about the other issues become more vocal in opposing abortion? Perhaps, just perhaps, we'd make a lot of progress in promoting the culture of life, defeating the culture of death and changing the outcome of the next poll taken in Catholic Rhode Island.

CHAPTER 2

Respecting Life,
a Year-Round Commitment

October is Respect Life Month, a time of special programs and prayers aimed at promoting respect for human life in our nation. Throughout the Diocese of Providence many parishes, schools and organizations will host very special events to proclaim the Gospel of Life in the midst of our culture of death. To all those involved in this important cause, I extend my profound gratitude, prayers and blessings.

But while October has been designated Respect Life Month, we know that the crusade on behalf of human life has to be a year-round commitment. As I've said so often, protecting human life is the great moral challenge of our time. I'm convinced that future generations will look back and judge us on that singular question: What did we do to preserve and promote human life when it was being attacked on so many fronts? As Disciples of Christ and members of the Church it is our inescapable duty to respond to the challenge and stand up for life!

Human life is such a precious gift of God, and yet so sadly, our society has become very casual in its approach.

Each year I spend a couple of weeks in Florida, along the beautiful southwest coast near Ft. Myers. As I stroll along the beach, especially in the summer, I often see little mounds of sand, carefully roped-off, indicating the presence of a sea turtle nest. A stern sign placed nearby cautions passersby not to disturb the nest because unborn sea turtles are protected by federal law. Harming unborn sea turtles could result in fines and imprisonment, the sign warns.

How sad and ironic it is, I reflect while walking, that unborn sea turtles are protected by federal law while unborn children aren't. I can go to jail for disturbing a little turtle, but if I kill a child in the womb, there's no consequence. Obviously something has gone terribly awry in our society.

The sad truth is that human life has become just another commodity, casually discarded if it becomes inconvenient for us. If someone else's existence interferes in our goals, our plans, or our personal needs, we just destroy it, invoking the abused principles of freedom and choice. That's the agenda that drives abortion, embryonic stem cell research, assisted suicide, capital punishment, domestic and urban violence, and international terrorism. All these sins against life are related and the thread that ties them together is the destruction of life for the sake of a personal agenda.

As a society we've got to learn that we can't solve our problems by ending human life! And for us as people of life, there are at least three things to do.

First, we must check our own personal attitudes, our thoughts, words and deeds. While we need to engage the secular culture about life, the commitment to life begins with you and me. Is our commitment to human life consistent? Do we make exceptions to meet our own agendas? Do we give good example to others in witnessing to life?

Secondly, our commitment to life should lead us to become politically involved. And I don't mean, necessarily, that we need to line up on one side of the partisan divide or the other. I don't give a whit if you're a Democrat, Republican, Independent or anything else. Your involvement in the political arena should be for the sole purpose of effecting sound laws and promoting the common good. The Church has defined this as the proper role of the laity – to transform the secular order into the Kingdom of God.

But that's where I get confused. If Rhode Island is the "most Catholic" state in the nation, as we hear so often, why do we keep electing public officials who support abortion? Is your party affiliation more important than your commitment to life? Have you ever voted for a candidate who supports "abortion rights" (or "freedom of choice" as it's usually rationalized)? If so, you're part of the problem, my friend, and you bear at least some responsibility for the culture of death in which we live. Think about it.

Finally, in our commitment to life we have to believe in the power of prayer. The struggle for human life is, at its root, a moral struggle, a spiritual struggle. While we work to change laws, we know that only God can change hearts. And so we need to pray and ask for God's blessing and assistance. We need to receive the Sacraments of the Church, the ultimate source of our spiritual strength. And we need to follow the example of our Blessed Mother, Our Lady of Life, who, despite difficult personal circumstances, recognized, cherished and protected the unborn life in her womb as a precious gift of God.

Summarizing our firm commitment to human life, the Bishops of the United States have written: "May we never tire of proclaiming the dignity and worth of every human life. May we never tire of serving the vulnerable and their caregivers with generous hearts. And may we never cease to pray for the day when all people, and all societies, will defend the life of every human from conception to natural death."

CHAPTER 3

Civil Rights and Human Life

Compared to the busyness and excitement of December, January is a rather quiet month. The holidays are behind us and we've settled in to survive the onslaught of winter, whether it turns out to be a lion or a lamb.

But there are two observances in January that demand our special attention – the celebration of the birthday of Dr. Martin Luther King, Jr., and the annual observance of the infamous Supreme Court decision, *Roe v. Wade*. And while the two events are distinct, they do have something in common.

January 15 marks the birthday of Martin Luther King, Baptist minister and great civil rights leader. Each year at this time there's a variety of worship services, community programs and educational initiatives aimed at remembering the man and promoting his message. The holiday has special meaning for the African-American community but the virtues we lift up that day should have significance for us all – virtues such as human dignity, equal opportunity and basic civil rights.

Without a doubt the most famous event of Dr. King's life was the August 28, 1963 March on Washington and his "I Have a Dream" speech. The speech has a privileged place in American history but more importantly lives on as a challenge for our own day.

In part Dr. King said, "I have a dream that one day this nation will rise up and live out the true meaning of its creed: 'We hold these truths to be self-evident, that all men are created equal.'"

And again, "With this faith we will be able to hew out of the mountain of despair a stone of hope. With this faith we will be able to transform the jangling discords of our nation into a beautiful symphony of brotherhood."

And again, "Let freedom ring . . . When we let it ring from every village and every hamlet, from every state and every city, we will be able to speed up the day when all of God's children – black men and white men, Jews and Gentiles, Protestants and Catholics – will be able to join hands and sing in the words of the old Negro spiritual: 'Free at last! Free at last! Thank God Almighty, we are free at last!'"

The civil rights movement in our country has made significant progress since Dr. King's rousing call to action, but we know there is still much more to do. The dream is alive, but not yet fulfilled.

The other event we observe (though surely not celebrate) in January is the dastardly Supreme Court decision, *Roe v. Wade*, that effectively removed every legal protection from human beings prior to birth. Its tragic legacy is death and sorrow.

The American Bishops have pointed out the devastating consequences of *Roe v. Wade*: the death of millions of babies whose lives were destroyed before birth and even during the very process of being born; countless women traumatized by the violence of abortion; men who grieve because they had no "choice" about the survival of their children; and a society marred by a pervasive lack of respect for human life in all of its manifestations. (USCCB, *Pastoral Plan for Pro-Life Activities*)

Several years after *Roe v. Wade* Blessed Mother Teresa of Calcutta, witnessing from afar the moral decline of America, wrote to the Supreme Court: "America needs no words from me to see how your decision in *Roe v. Wade* has deformed a great nation. The so-called right to abortion has pitted mothers against their children and women against men. It has sown violence and discord at the heart of the most intimate of human relationships."

Thirty-five years after the Supreme Court decision the attack on human life is as relentless and insidious as ever, assuming new tactics, it seems, all the time. The battle for human life continues to be the great struggle of our time, the singular moral question on which future generations will judge our own. Every Catholic worthy of the name, indeed every person concerned about the moral law and the common good, must be committed to the protection and defense of human life, beginning with (though not ending at) the protection of innocent, unborn children.

Civil rights and human life. While they are distinct causes, they share something very important: They both presume the dignity of the human person. As the Bishops of the United States have explained: "Every human person is created in the image and likeness of God . . . Calls to advance human rights are illusions if the right to life itself is subject to attack." (*Faithful Citizenship, 1999*)

It follows then, that if you're committed to the civil rights movement you should also be passionate about protecting the life of unborn children. And likewise, if you're dedicated to the pro-life movement, you have a concomitant obligation to promote civil rights for all of God's children.

Civil rights and human life are the twin virtues, the building blocks on which a decent America must be built. January – with the birthday of Martin Luther King and the observance of *Roe v. Wade* – is a perfect time to rediscover that link and recommit ourselves to the cause.

CHAPTER 4

Why "Gay Marriage" Is Wrong

Why is the Church so adamantly opposed to "gay marriages" and civil unions? Doesn't the Church's stance discriminate against homosexuals? What harm is done if homosexual activity is between consenting adults? How does it affect my marriage and family? Why does the Church care if in fact the Church won't be required to witness such unions?

These are just some of the questions bantered about today in the debate over gay marriage and civil unions. (And for the sake of the record, there's really no difference between the two; just different terms for the same thing. It seems, however, that some advocates use civil unions as a stepping stone to legitimize gay marriage.)

As the debate continues, it's really important that Catholics understand why this is such a critical moral issue and why the Church is involved. And we begin with a review of the Church's fundamental teaching about marriage.

As Catholics we believe that matrimony is a sacred institution, designed by God and raised to a level of a sacrament by Jesus Christ.

God created man in his image; in the divine image he created him; male and female he created them. God blessed them, saying: "Be fertile and multiply; fill the earth and subdue it. Have dominion over the fish of the sea, the birds of the air, and all the living things that move on the earth." (Gn 1:27-28)

The teaching of the Church explains: "The intimate community of life and love which constitutes the married state has been established by the Creator and endowed by him with its own proper laws . . . God himself is the author of marriage." (*Catechism of the Catholic Church, #1603*)

The two divinely established purposes of marriage are obvious – to promote life and love – to be creative and unitive. This life-giving complementarity between the sexes is natural and normative. "Holy Scripture affirms that man and woman were created for one another." (*Catechism, #1604*)

A statement of the Pontifical Council for the Family, *Family, Marriage and De Facto Unions*, explains it this way: "We can also see how incongruous is the demand to grant 'marital' status to unions between persons of the same sex. It is opposed, first of all, by the objective impossibility of making the partnership fruitful through the transmission of life according to the plan inscribed by God . . . Marriage cannot be reduced to a condition similar to that of a homosexual relationship: this is contrary to common sense." *(#23)*

The statement refers to "common sense" and I think that's important. When we learned about the birds and the bees, it was always male and female birds and bees, wasn't it? Some advocates of homosexuality point to the fact that there's evidence of homosexual behavior in the animal kingdom, and I suppose that's true. But it always emerges as an exception to the norm, doesn't it?

Finally, even from a biological standpoint, the "facts of life" are obvious: man and woman are physically designed for union with each other.

In short, from the evidence of the Bible, the teachings of the Church, common sense and biology, so called gay marriages and civil unions are contrary to God's plan, morally objectionable, and an unacceptable substitute for marriage.

But how do we respond to the questions being raised today?

Isn't the Church's teaching discriminatory against homosexuals?

Not at all. The Church's teaching about homosexuality should be well known by now. It revolves around the distinction between homosexual *activity* and homosexual *persons*. First is the Church's belief that "Homosexual acts are intrinsically disordered. They are contrary to the natural law . . . Under no circumstances can they be approved." (*Catechism*, #2357) The Church also insists, however, that men and women with same sex attractions are valued members of the human family and must be treated with the same respect and love as every other child of God. "Every sign of unjust discrimination in their regard should be avoided." (*Catechism*, #2358) As I've publicly written on two other occasions, "Hatred, persecution, prejudice and ridicule of homosexuals is a grave sin and must always be treated as such." (*The Catholic Exponent*, November 14, 1997 and November 8, 2002.)

This teaching of the Church does not intend to offend our homosexual brothers and sisters, and we recognize that for some individuals and their families, especially parents, questions of sexual identity and behavior can be very difficult and emotionally charged. To those individuals and their families we offer our sincere concern and prayerful support. As a society, however, we have to understand the possibility, sometimes the necessity, of loving and respecting individuals even while rejecting their inappropriate or immoral behavior. (Parents have to do that with their children once in awhile, don't they?)

Additionally, it's not a matter of civil rights as some have claimed. Freedom is not unbridled license. Authentic human freedom is intrinsically connected to moral truth. In short, there's never a right to do something wrong.

What harm is done if the activity is between consenting adults?

The fact that two adults consent to an action doesn't make it morally right or socially acceptable. The "harm" is that such reasoning leads us down a very dangerous and permissive slope to the detriment of the common good and the spiritual impoverishment of the individuals involved. After all, two consenting adults can engage in drug use, prostitution, bigamy, polygamy or other immoral activities. In other words, the determination of the morality of an action is found in the act itself and not in the consent of the people involved!

How does "gay marriage" affect my marriage and family?

We should recognize that in every culture and society throughout the ages traditionally defined marriage, as a stable union of one man and one woman, has been normative and has been given protection and respect. "The definition of the family's identity is a priority. . . . Such marital and family stability does not only depend on the good will of concrete persons; it takes on an institutional character of public recognition by the state. . . The recognition, protection and promotion of this stability contributes to the general interest, especially of the weakest, i.e., the children." (*Family, Marriage and De Facto Unions, #14*)

In other, simpler terms, marriage as traditionally defined has always been a privileged institution, and that distinction should be recognized, preserved and applauded. Accepting other personal unions as equivalent to marriage undermines the special status afforded to marriage in every society and culture. Examples of this point: in the classroom if all the students routinely get A's on their report card, the work of the real A student is devalued. In the Olympics, if everyone receives a gold medal, why bother competing? And if everything is marriage, then marriage is nothing!

Why does the Church care if in fact the Church won't be required to preside over such unions?

First of all the Church is a citizen of this world and cares deeply about the moral condition of the culture in which she lives as well as the spiritual well-being of all our brothers and sisters, Catholic and non-Catholic alike.

More to the point however, recent experience has shown that practices that begin as optional quickly become mandatory, even for religious communities morally opposed to them. Recall, for example, that in Massachusetts, there has been a concerted effort to require Catholic adoption agencies to place children with homosexual "families" although such a practice is clearly opposed to Catholic moral principles. In some states there has been a move to force Catholic health care facilities to provide "emergency contraception" or other immoral procedures, even when they are contrary to the sacred holdings of their conscience.

Is there much doubt, therefore, that before long some activists, appealing to the argument of "non-discrimination" will seek to require the Catholic Church to witness or approve of gay marriages or civil unions under the threat of civil or even criminal penalties?

Finally, a word about our political leaders. Legislators have a serious moral obligation to preserve and promote the common good; to support laws that protect marriage and family and reject legislative initiatives that fail to do so.

The statement from the Pontifical Council for the Family explains, "Those who are involved in politics ought to be aware of the seriousness of this problem . . . It is up to politicians to be vigilant (not only on the level of principles but also of applications) to avoid a breakdown, with serious present and future consequences, of the relationship between moral and civil law." (#18) And as Pope John Paul II said, in words that surely apply to this question: "No one can ever renounce this responsibility, especially when he or she has a legislative or decision-making mandate, which calls that person to answer to God, to his or her own conscience and to the whole of society." (*Evangelium Vitae*, #90)

Our legislators are under intense political pressure from well-organized special interest groups to support legislative initiatives that would obliterate traditional concepts of marriage and family. Our representatives need our prayers, as well as our personal and public support, that they will have the wisdom to know what is right and the courage to do it in protecting the precious gift of marriage and family.

To summarize: We believe that matrimony is a sacred union of one man and one woman, designed by God and blessed by Jesus Christ, and that it is a fundamental building block of every society and culture. We believe that persons with homosexual tendencies are children of God and our brothers and sisters, deserving of our respect and prayers. We believe, however, that homosexual activity is immoral, that it is contrary to the natural law, the tenets of the Bible and the teaching of the Church. We believe that the concept of gay marriage or civil unions detracts from the common good and is harmful to families, and that the state should not, and in fact cannot, ratify such unions.

"God created man in his image, in the divine image he created him; male and female he created them. God blessed them saying, "Be fertile and multiply; fill the earth and subdue it." Genesis 1:27-28

CHAPTER 5

Immigrants Are People, Not Problems

"I was a stranger and you welcomed me." (Mt 25:35)

In a time when both the community and the Church are trying to respond to a new wave of immigrants, these words of Jesus should inspire a serious examination of conscience for us all. It's an important exercise because Jesus reminds us that the way we welcome "strangers" will serve as one of the criteria for our final judgment. It's also important to ensure that our nation remains true to its better instincts and the Church to the inclusive spirit of Christ.

So, a question: Do you see immigrants as blessings or burdens, people to be welcomed or problems to be solved?

A few years ago, the American Bishops issued a statement on immigration entitled *Welcoming the Stranger Among Us*. In light of the sometimes fierce debate taking place today, it might be helpful to revisit the Bishops' document. It makes several important points.

For example, the document reminds us that most of us "Americans" have immigrant pasts, and that our Catholic ancestors also faced hardships and persecution. For that reason we should be especially sensitive to any form of discrimination against newcomers today. "Perhaps the greatest obstacle to welcoming the stranger is that many Americans have forgotten their immigrant past. 'Nativism' assumes that there is just one image of a 'real American' and that immigrants either cannot live up to it or willfully refuse to do so."

The statement addresses the thorny question of "undocumented immigrants." First, it explains that the Church does not condone undocumented migration, and it emphasizes that "nations have the right to control their borders." Most people would agree, I think, that clear and consistent immigration policies, along with careful control of our national borders, are very reasonable goals.

But the Bishops go on to affirm that "the Church supports the human rights of all people and offers them pastoral care, education and social services, no matter the circumstances of entry into this country."

In a time when our nation is increasingly tempted to isolate itself and seal its borders, and the state, for fiscal purposes, threatens to eliminate critical social services for the undocumented and their children, it's good to recall that immigrants, regardless of the paper they carry or don't, are children of God and brothers and sisters to us. Though our resources are limited, we have a moral mandate to properly order our priorities and make a communal commitment to assist newcomers and respond to their social, educational, and health-care needs.

The public debate over immigration in our society and its consequences is certainly legitimate. Sometimes, however, the rhetoric heard on radio talk shows and found in letters to the editor takes an ugly, mean-spirited, even ominous tone. The Bishops deal with that problem, too, and strongly reject "the anti-immigrant stance that has become popular in different parts of our country, and the nativism, ethnocentricity, and racism that continue to reassert themselves."

Immigrants have spiritual needs too and the Church also has to examine its own conscience in this area. The Bishops teach: "The call to communion goes out to all members of the Church – bishops, priests, deacons, religious, lay leaders, and parishioners – to prepare themselves to receive newcomers with a genuine spirit of welcome. Simple, grace-filled kindness and concern on the part of all parishioners to newcomers are the first steps." The document adds, "Both on parish and diocesan levels, the presence of brothers and sisters from different cultures should be celebrated as a gift to the Church."

I warmly commend the parishes, schools and institutions of the Diocese of Providence, along with members of diocesan staff, who for a long time now have been fully committed to welcoming immigrants, assisting them, responding to their needs, and integrating them into the life of the Church. This noble ministry will continue to be a priority for our local Church.

In that spirit, I suggest several things that all the members of the Catholic community can do on behalf of our immigrants.

First, we can examine our own attitudes about the immigrants in our nation and community. Are our thoughts, words and deeds worthy of the spirit of Christ or are they sometimes much less than that – negative, harsh, even sinful?

Second, we can take practical steps to ensure that newcomers are kindly received and warmly welcomed into our neighborhoods, parishes, schools and institutions. And while we respond to their needs we should also gratefully receive the gifts they bring to the table. Without a doubt, in due time, the new immigrants, like those of past generations, will strengthen our union, contribute to our community and enrich our culture.

Third, we can support the reform of legislation so that it assists in a comprehensive and generous manner the immigrants who come to our country; and support federal and state budgets that provide sufficient funding to meet their basic human needs.

Finally, we can pray everyday for those who are newcomers to our country and our Church; for their safety, health and prosperity; and that our new neighbors will find full communion with us, "the communion willed by God, begun in time and destined for completion in the fullness of the Kingdom." (*Ecclesia in America, #33*)

"*I was a stranger and you welcomed me.*" What do those words mean for you? Think about it.

CHAPTER 6

My R.S.V.P. to Rudy Giuliani

I probably would have written this article anyhow, so distressed was I. But then I received an invitation to attend a fundraising luncheon for presidential candidate Rudy Giuliani, and that absolutely confirmed my decision. The fundraiser is scheduled for Providence next week. For $500 I could attend a reception with the former New York City mayor. For $1,500 I could attend a reception with a photo op. The first thought that came to my mind is that I'm not charging enough for my Confirmation photos!

Nevertheless, and more to the point, I have no idea why I received an invitation to Giuliani's fundraiser. I don't know the mayor; I've never met him. I try to avoid partisan politics. Heck, I'm not even a Republican. But most of all, I would never support a candidate who supports legalized abortion.

Rudy's public proclamations on abortion are pathetic and confusing. Even worse, they're hypocritical.

Now this is what we get from Rudy as he attempted to explain his ambiguous position on abortion in a speech at Houston Baptist College earlier this month: "Here are the two strong beliefs that I have, here are the two pillars of my thinking . . . One is, I believe abortion is wrong. I think it is morally wrong . . . The second pillar that guides my thinking . . . where [people of good faith] come to different conclusions about this, about something so very, very personal, I believe you have to respect their viewpoint. You give them a level of choice here . . . I've always believed both of these things."

What? This drivel from the man who received high marks, and properly so, for his clear vision and personal courage in healing New York City, and by extension, the nation, after the horrific terrorist attacks of September 11?

Rudy mentions the two pillars of his position. But you know what happens if you sit on a stool with two legs? Yep, it collapses. And so does Rudy's position and along with it his integrity and reputation.

Rudy's explanation is a classic expression of the position on abortion we've heard from weak-kneed politicians so frequently in recent years: "I'm personally opposed to but don't want to impose my views on other people." The incongruity of that position has been exposed many times now. As I've asked previously, would we let any politician get away with the same pathetic cop-out on other issues: "I'm personally opposed to . . . racial discrimination, sexual abuse, prostitution, drug abuse, polygamy, incest . . . but don't want to impose my beliefs on others?"

Why is it that when I hear someone explaining this position I think of the sad figure of Pontius Pilate in the Gospels who personally found no guilt in Jesus but for fear of the crowd washed his hands of the whole affair and handed Jesus over to be crucified. I can just hear Pilate saying, "You know, I'm personally opposed to crucifixion but don't want to impose my belief on others."

Okay, let's ask Mayor Giuliani to think about his position for a minute.

Hey Rudy, you say that you believe abortion is morally wrong. Why do you say that Rudy, why do you believe that abortion is wrong? Is abortion the killing of an innocent child? Is it an offense against human dignity? Is it a cruel and violent act? Does it harm the woman who has the abortion? And if your answer to any of these questions is yes, Rudy, why would you permit people to . . . kill an innocent child, offend human dignity, commit a cruel and violent act or do harm to the mother? This in the name of choice? Huh?

Rudy's preposterous position is compounded by the fact that he professes to be a Catholic. As Catholics we are called, indeed required, to be pro-life, to cherish and protect human life as a precious gift of God from the moment of conception until the time of natural death. As a leader, as public official, Rudy Giuliani has a special obligation in that regard.

In *The Gospel of Life* Pope John Paul II made the obligation to defend human life very explicit: "This task is the particular responsibility of civil leaders . . . No one can ever renounce this responsibility, especially when he or she has a legislative or decision-making mandate." (#90) And more recently, the Bishops of the United States wrote: "If a Catholic in his or her personal or professional life were knowingly and obstinately to repudiate [the Church's] definitive teaching on moral issues, he or she would seriously diminish his or her communion with the Church." (*Happy Are Those Who Are Called to His Supper*, p. 11)

Rudy's defection from the Catholic Faith on this moral issue is not unique, of course. Catholic politicians of both parties, nationwide, have followed a similar path in abandoning the faith for the sake of political expediency:

Ted Kennedy, John Kerry, Pat Leahy, Nancy Pelosi, and Joe Biden come quickly to mind. And on a local level of course, Congressman Patrick Kennedy and Senator Jack Reed. How these intelligent men and women will someday stand before the judgment seat of God and explain why they legitimized the death of countless innocent children in the sin of abortion is beyond me. ("But God, really, I was personally opposed to it but just couldn't do anything about it.")

Oh well, as you can see by now, I won't be attending the fundraiser for Rudy Giuliani. If Rudy wants to see me he'll have to arrange an appointment at my office. We'll talk about his position on abortion. And if he wants a photo it will cost him $1,500 as a donation for the pro-life work of the Church.

CHAPTER 7

Racism: It's Bigger Than Imus

Racism is a sin: a sin that divides the human family, blots out the image of God among specific members of that family, and violates the fundamental human dignity of those called to be children of the same Father. (USCCB Statement, "Brothers and Sisters to Us")

Without a doubt you've been following, or at least heard about, the recent news story involving the nationally syndicated radio talk show host, Don Imus, and his verbal attack on the Rutgers University women's basketball team. His words were gratuitous, vulgar and insulting. As a result he was fired. Good.

The only thing that surprised me about the story is that Imus was fired now and not a long time ago. After all, he built his whole career on outrageous and offensive comments. He routinely insulted African-Americans, Jews, Catholics, women and homosexuals. But it didn't seem to bother his fans. He had a loyal following and he made lots of money for his employers. That was enough, apparently, to shield him from negative reactions to previous rantings.

This time, though, he went too far and pushed the wrong buttons.

The Imus episode, important as it is, opens the door to a broader discussion and points to a persistent evil in the human family: racism. The USCCB statement quoted above begins with these words: "Racism is an evil which endures in our society and in our Church. Despite apparent advances and even significant changes in the last two decades, the reality of racism remains."

One has to wonder if we'll ever outgrow the sin of racism or if it's an inherent trait of the human family.

I remember hearing the story of a school bus driver who drove both white and black school children in his bus every day. Regularly the journey to school was marred by taunting and fighting along racial lines. The driver quickly tired of the fighting and one day decreed to the children: "Beginning tomorrow there will be no more white children and no more black children on this bus. Beginning tomorrow, we'll all be green!" The driver was proud of his solution to the burgeoning social challenge and thought that the problem was solved. Until the next day, when one little boy got on the bus and declared, "Okay guys, light green in the back; dark green in the front."

In searching for evidence of racism, though, often one has to look no further than the mirror. Few of us, it seems, are completely immune to racism. Including me.

A number of years ago, I stopped to get gas in Ohio when a car pulled up behind me with the radio blasting, the bass thumping, and the refrigerator-sized speakers vibrating everything on the street. "Why," I asked myself, "are these young black guys always so arrogant?" "Why do they have to inflict their obnoxious music on everyone else?" At which point I turned around and saw this skinny little white kid with blond hair and blue eyes getting out of his car. At that moment I recognized the ugly racism in my heart. I was embarrassed; I asked the Lord for forgiveness and resolved that in the future I would always try to avoid categorizing and stereotyping groups of people.

Overt expressions of racism are usually frowned upon today and aren't socially acceptable. But more subtle expressions of racism persist. I wonder, for example, if the vehement anti-immigrant feelings found in some individuals are fueled, at least *sometimes*, by the bias against those with darker skin. The prejudice might not be intentional; it might be subconscious or subliminal, but it's real nonetheless.

And while most prejudice is leveled against those with different skin color, its ugly first-cousin is found in anti-Semitism. Prejudice against Jews is ignorant and evil, contrary to the law of love and Gospel of Christ. Any remnant of it in society or the Church needs to be eradicated. The Bishops of the Second Vatican Council made it very clear: "[The Church] deplores all hatreds, persecutions, displays of anti-Semitism leveled at any time or from any source against the Jews." (*Nostra Aetate*, #4)

In this context it's important to note too, that at least in some quarters, prejudice against Christians and Catholics continues to be acceptable, even fashionable. One can only hope that the mainstream media, social activists and general population will challenge and reject anti-Christian and anti-Catholic expressions with the same determination with which they reject other prejudices today. (You think Imus would have been fired if he had insulted Catholics?)

Racism can be found in every nation and among every people of the world and routinely results in discrimination, persecution, suffering and war. It's as universal as it is deplorable. And it can affect relations among nations. As the Bishops' statement observes, "Globally, we live in an interdependent community of nations, some rich, some poor . . . Racial difference should not interfere with our dealing justly and peacefully with all other nations."

While we can't forget, then, the global consequences of racism, the real battleground in overcoming prejudice begins much closer to home, by looking into our own heart and soul. Remember the proverb: "If everyone swept in front of his own door, soon the whole world would be clean."

As children of God and followers of Christ let's get rid of racism. It's a sin, "a sin that divides the human family and blots out the image of God."

CHAPTER 8

Questions about the Casino

In reviewing my files I see that it's been almost ten years since I've written about gambling. In light of the fierce debate that took place in Rhode Island prior to the 2004 elections, I thought it was an opportune time to revisit the question.

First, a word about the Church's approach to gambling. The Catholic Church does *not* hold that all gambling is immoral. There is no Scriptural, traditional or magisterial basis for such a teaching. *The Catechism of the Catholic Church* explains: "Games of chance (card games, etc.) or wagers are not in themselves contrary to justice. They become morally unacceptable when they deprive someone what is necessary to provide for his needs and those of others. The passion for gambling risks becoming enslavement." (#2413)

In other words, while gambling itself is morally neutral, the circumstances surrounding it can render it immoral. These circumstances include: using excessive amounts of money, addiction to gambling, gambling that is unfair to the participants, gambling that leads to crime and corruption, as well as gambling that causes collateral damage to individuals, families, or communities.

Gambling is a very sensitive topic for Catholics. We realize that there are moral concerns about gambling, but still we play bingo, sell raffle tickets, have parish festivals with games of chance, and organize trips to Atlantic City and Las Vegas. Are sins being committed every time these activities take place? I don't think so.

In the interest of full disclosure it should be noted that Yours Truly has been known to participate in a little gambling on occasion. I buy raffle tickets to support a local parish or school. I participate in friendly football pools. I've won and lost (usually lost) a few bucks on the golf course. And on a few occasions I've even made a pilgrimage to Foxwoods, paying my tithe to the slot machines. (A word of self-defense: In light of my Irish-German heritage and very frugal nature, both the time and money spent there are always strictly limited!)

Gambling can have useful purposes. Gambling provides funds for non-profit agencies such as churches, schools and fire departments. It can be relaxing and fun for a group of friends. It can entice people out of their homes and form local communities. Many of our senior citizens find their primary social support around bingo tables.

It strikes me that as Catholics our approach to gambling is very similar to our approach to alcohol. While drinking alcohol is not evil in itself, the morality is found in the circumstances of its use or abuse.

We should be very reluctant then to level a universal condemnation of gambling. There is no theology to support such a stance and we can easily be accused of being hypocritical on the issue.

Even with that starting point, however, there are important questions to consider.

The rapid proliferation and acceptance of gambling in our society is troublesome. But if you've ever purchased a lottery ticket or participated in the annual football pool at the office you've contributed to that trend. Some have even suggested that "playing" the stock market is a form of gambling. After all, isn't it an investment of money with the chance of winning or losing very "iffy?"

The fact that the culture of gambling is ensnaring many of our young people, including college and high school students, is a growing and serious problem.

Without a doubt, large scale, corporate, professional gambling – such as that found in casinos – is in league of its own. It's essentially different from the gambling already mentioned and it presents serious concerns. This form of gambling is far more dangerous to individuals, families and communities. More money is involved. It's more addictive. Its primary motive is profit, not charity.

So, as we debate the development of a casino in Rhode Island, it's appropriate to reflect upon a few questions.

- In light of the proximity of other casinos in our region do we really need another one closer to home?
- Is corporate gambling the best we can do for economic development?
- Do the anticipated short-term benefits justify the potential long-term liabilities the gambling environment creates?
- Will a significant portion of the proceeds be dedicated to some redeeming social value, such as tax reduction, education or assistance to the poor?
- Are we sure that gambling will not engender other unsavory activities such as organized crime, prostitution or use of drugs?
- Is the participation of minors prohibited?

- Will there be sufficient supervision to ensure that the games are fair and that cheating is not involved?

These and perhaps other criteria need to be considered in evaluating the development of any casino gambling effort.

Nevertheless, the decision whether or not to support a specific casino – in a particular place, developed by a particular company, for the benefit of a particular group – is not a moral issue. It's a practical, prudential judgment about which people of goodwill might come to different conclusions.

CHAPTER 9

The Church Has Been Green for a Long Time

Remember when green was just a color, like red or blue or black or white? It's so much more than that now. Green has become a political party, a sociological movement, and even a moral commitment. It's all about the environment of course, and the issue is way up there at the top of the hot button list along with the war in Iraq, gay marriage and illegal immigration.

Want to start a lively discussion? Just ask a few people what they think about global warming. Chances are the opinions will vary widely and the discussion itself will heat up enough to contribute to the warming of the atmosphere. It's an issue that has resurrected the dormant career of former Vice President Al Gore, who has traveled the world warning about the effects of global warming, all the while encouraging others to travel less and reduce their consumption of fossil fuel.

The burning question (excuse the pun) is this: Is global warming the result of the normal cycle of nature, experienced periodically during the earth's history, or the result of unprecedented and uncontrolled human activity? According to some dire predictions, if the warming of the earth continues unabated, glaciers will melt, animals will migrate to unusual habitats, hurricanes will intensify to deadly proportions, and the climate in Providence will soon rival that of Puerto Rico. I'm sure that scientists and politicians will continue the debate, and that liberals and conservatives will continue to throw verbal stones at each other across the ecological divide.

Personally, I suspect that global warming is a lethal mélange of both factors — the recurring cycles of nature and destructive human activity. It seems to me, then, that in approaching the question of global warming and the broader issue of the environment we need to strike a balance — to avoid hysteria but approach the question deliberately and seriously.

Political jockeying aside, the protection of the environment is a very serious moral issue, one that the Church has addressed for a long time, long before it became the issue-du-jour. Consider the following . . .

"The seventh commandment enjoins respect for the integrity of creation . . . Man's dominion over inanimate and other living beings granted by the Creator is not absolute; it is limited by concern for the quality of life of his neighbor, including generations to come; it requires a religious respect for the integrity of creation." (*The Catechism of the Catholic Church, #2415*)

"To men and women, the crown of the entire process of creation, the Creator entrusts the care of the earth. This brings concrete obligations in the areas of ecology for every person . . . All people of good will must work to ensure the effective protection of the environment, understood as a gift of God." (Pope John Paul II, *The Church in America, #25)*

"The continuing debate about how the United States is responding to the questions and challenges surrounding global climate change is a test and an opportunity for our nation and the entire Catholic community . . . At its core, global climate change is not about economic theory or political platforms, nor about partisan advantage or interest group pressures. It is about the future of God's creation and the one human family." (United States Catholic Bishops, *Global Climate Change*.)

The Vatican is leading the way and becoming greener. The Paul VI Centre (the audience hall) is getting an environmentally friendly makeover with the installation of a giant rooftop garden of solar panels that will power all of the building's heating, cooling and lighting needs year-round.

And Pope Benedict XVI himself, while still wearing white, has become green. In responding to a question presented to him recently, the Pope said: "We can all see today that man could destroy the foundation of his existence, the earth. Therefore we can no longer just simply do whatever we want with this earth which has been entrusted to us. We must respect the inner law of creation, of the earth, to learn these laws and obey these laws if we are to survive." The Pope went on to speak of "obedience to the voice of the earth," a neat little phrase that places concern for the environment in the context of the natural law.

For his environmental sensitivity, including his use of an electric-powered popemobile, Pope Benedict has been ranked as one of the top green religious leaders in the world by the online environmental magazine, *Grist*. "When he speaks out on an issue, the world listens," said the editor of *Grist*.

The protection of the environment is a legitimate moral question. It's an issue that should spark interest and inspire discussion in our diocese and our parishes, schools and organizations. We need to ask if there are effective ways in which we, as an institution, can promote a healthy environment. But in the end, like so many other things, it begins with you and me. What are you doing (and what am I doing) to preserve the beautiful home God has given us?

"God looked at everything He had made and found it very good." (Gn 1:31) That divine perspective of creation should be enough to inspire us to take the question seriously.

CHAPTER 10

When Faith and Work Collide

A number of years ago, when I was still serving as a parish priest, a gentleman approached me with a very serious moral dilemma.

He explained that he was working as a projectionist in a local movie house and that until recently he had enjoyed his job, and that it was meeting his personal and financial needs. But then new owners purchased the theater, and they wanted to change the atmosphere and attract new clientele. To do so, they began showing pornographic movies. This presented a crisis of conscience for the projectionist.

He explained, "Father Tobin, I need my job to support me and my wife. I'm sixty years old. If I quit this job, it's very unlikely that I'll find something else that's suitable for me and pays enough. But I'm a good Catholic and I really feel guilty about showing these filthy movies. I know it's wrong, but I really don't know if I can afford to lose my job. What should I do?"

I told this good man, first of all, that I admired his concern in even asking the question. I told him that the decision was his and his alone, that no one could make it for him. I also suggested that he would need a lot of moral courage to do what is right, but that ultimately his personal integrity and peace of mind would be far more important than the modest paycheck he took home each week.

A few months later I ran into the man again. He told me that he had quit his job at the theater, had found other work that was paying him more, and that he was proud of himself, happy and peaceful!

The lesson here is that nothing in life is more important than religious faith, for it defines our relationship with Almighty God, our Creator and Judge.

That's a worthwhile point to remember these days when we see the sad spectacle of Catholic politicians doing just the opposite – betraying their faith for the sake of political gain. This happens especially as they tiptoe around the abortion issue. How often have we heard a Catholic politician whimper, "I'm personally opposed to abortion but don't want to impose my beliefs on others?" It's just so disappointing. Would we let a politician escape with the same pathetic cop-out on other issues: "I'm personally opposed . . . to racial discrimination, to sexual abuse, to child pornography . . . but don't want to impose my beliefs on others?"

How far we've moved from the stirring example of a great Catholic politician, St. Thomas More, who gave his life rather than betray his faith. In the play, *A Man for All Seasons*, St. Thomas More remarks, "I believe, when statesmen forsake their own private conscience for the sake of their public duties, they lead their country by a short route to chaos." And as he went to his execution, he proclaimed without hesitation, "I die the king's good servant, but God's first."

Today, as much as ever, we need the leadership of Catholic politicians imbued with the spirit of Thomas

More. We need leaders who are principled and courageous, not ambiguous and cowardly.

Along these same lines it's important to remember that other Catholics often find themselves in similar circumstances where the expectations of their work challenge the priority of their faith.

- What about Catholic doctors and nurses expected to perform or assist with abortions?
- What about Catholic entertainers asked to participate in morally offensive performances?
- What about Catholic CEOs expected to engage in unethical business practices?
- What about Catholic soldiers required to fight an unjust war?

In these, and in similar situations, the principle remains: Nothing in life is more important than religious faith, for it defines our relationship with Almighty God, our Creator and Judge.

Jesus explained the priority of faith this way: "If your hand causes you to sin, cut it off. It is better for you to enter into life maimed than with two hands to go into Gehenna, into the unquenchable fire. . . .And if your eye causes you to sin, pluck it out. Better for you to enter the kingdom of God with one eye than with two eyes to be thrown into Gehenna." (Mk 9: 43, 47)

So, what to do when faith and work collide? There's really no choice, is there? Quit your job and save your soul.

Faith and My Life

CHAPTER 11

The Real Blessings of Age

While I was Bishop of the Diocese of Youngstown, we sponsored several events for our senior citizens entitled "The Blessings of Age." On these occasions I invited older folks of the diocese to join me for a special Mass and reception. The program was arranged by Catholic Charities of the diocese and included the participation of some fine Catholic high school students who assisted with the liturgies and socials. The events were really enjoyable; a grand time was had by all!

The purpose of our gathering was to thank our senior citizens for their many contributions to the Church and community and to encourage them to keep up their good work. We also wanted to highlight the truth that every age of life is a gift of God to be treasured and celebrated. Thus the title, "The Blessings of Age."

Despite the positive tone of our celebrations, however, we recognize that not everybody grows old quite so willingly or gracefully. Surely Jack Benny is not the only person we know to have stopped counting at "39."

Speaking about age is usually considered to be impolite. A while back I came across a birthday card that said, on the outside, "I know it's impolite to ask a lady her age," and on the inside, "So, how much do you weigh?"

I remember friends of our family in Pittsburgh, an older couple, who fought and quarreled all the time. (Deep down they loved each other -they just had trouble expressing it!) In the midst of one particularly angry argument, the husband shouted to his wife, "You're nothing but a frustrated, old witch!" To which she fiercely retorted, "I am not old!" No objection to being a "frustrated witch" -but don't you dare call her "old."

In light of the difficulty some folks have growing old, then, I thought it would be a valuable public service if I collected for you the "real blessings of age," obviously not from a theological perspective, but rather, from the experience of everyday life!

10. When you reach a certain age, you get discounted prices on almost everything! Not that senior citizens don't deserve it, mind you, but they do get lots of breaks -in shops and stores, and for airline tickets, restaurants, movies, athletic events and even junkets to Las Vegas and Atlantic City. The discounts are so darn inviting, it's just not cost effective to die! You can't afford to miss out on the great savings that come your way simply by living a few extra years!

9. If you're a golfer, you get to play from the "gold tees" reserved for senior citizens, tees even closer to the greens than the ladies tees. The last time I played golf it was with a senior citizen who often hits the ball farther than I do. Nonetheless, he insisted on playing from the gold tees while I had to use the regular tees. More than once my drive, a good shot, took us to his approximate starting place. How fair is that? How old does one have to be to use the gold tees without a guilty conscience?

8. You can spoil your grandchildren and send them home to their parents. What grandparent hasn't had that temptation while entertaining their grandchildren? Buy the kids a special gift, let them stay up late at night, load them up with sugar before bedtime -and then return them to the discipline of their parents. It's perfect revenge for the pain and suffering grandparents endure while raising their kids!

7. You're no longer required to entertain and you're entitled to sponge off your family. For countless holiday meals and family gatherings you've done the shopping, cleaned the house, set the table, prepared the dinner, washed the dishes and cleaned the house all over again after the guests leave. But now you've paid your dues and earned your way. If you're over sixty-five and still entertaining, it's time to stop. This year, park yourself on someone else's doorstep for Thanksgiving and Christmas dinner- relax, enjoy yourself, fall asleep after dinner, say thank you, and go home!

6. You can use doggie bags in a restaurant without pretending to have a doggie. After all, it was senior citizens who made this practice fashionable years ago. Now, everybody does it. So many restaurants serve too much food at exorbitant prices. And as a golden ager who's lived through tough times, you appreciate the value of a good meal. No need to apologize, be embarrassed, or make up the name of your pooch at home. Just grab your Styrofoam container, fill it with leftover meatloaf, mashed potatoes, green beans and applesauce, and proudly stride out the door of the fashionable restaurant, knowing that your dinners for the next two days are just a few microwaved seconds away!

5. It's okay to watch reruns of your favorite TV shows without having to defend your taste in entertainment. It's safe to come out of the closet now -senior citizens are supposed to like "Lawrence Welk," "The Waltons," "Touched by an Angel," and "Mother Angelica Live." The first time around, you probably switched off the TV if someone came to visit while you were watching these shows. Now, your family and friends expect you to enjoy programs like that. However, if you're inclined to watch the "Victoria's Secret Fashion Show," MTV's "Real World," or the "Jerry Springer Show" keep your blinds closed! No need to scandalize the youngsters!

4. You're entitled to turn-off your hearing aid anytime you want to avoid unpleasant sounds. A loud family argument about politics or religion? Turn it off. The grandchildren running around the house making too much noise? Turn it off. (And refer to #8 above!) A boring sermon that's really irritating you? Turn it off. Your hearing aid is your friend. If you utilize the hearing aid option, however, be sure to turn it on again before you settle in to watch the "Lawrence Welk" rerun!

3. You can keep your family in line by threatening to write them out of your will. This is a sure-fire way to guarantee that your family will keep the rules, love you, respect you, and attend to your every need. A few points of strategy are important, however. Be sure to casually mention your will once in awhile, and wonder out loud if you should change any of the provisions. Above all, don't let your heirs know how much you've squirreled away. Give them the impression it's a lot. Sad to say, but their love and respect might be directly proportional to the amount of inheritance they think they'll receive!

2. You can blame a variety of mistakes on having a "senior moment." Lose your car keys around the house? Senior moment. Worse yet, lose your car in the parking lot? Senior moment. Forget your wife's name? Senior moment. Repeat the same story for the third time in an hour? Senior moment. Do any of these things after the age of sixty- five, it's a darling senior moment. Do the same things when you're younger, you're just plain stupid!

1. And, finally, the number one blessing of getting older... just forgot.

Anyhow, you can see how many advantages there are to growing older.

CHAPTER 12

Golfing with My Dad

Summer's a time for slowing down, kicking back, relaxing, and reminiscing. It's for that reason, perhaps, I've been thinking a lot about summers past, and especially one of my favorite pastimes in summers past, golfing with my dad. Though it's been 19 years now since my dad died, the memories of our golf outings remain crystal clear.

They usually took place on Wednesdays, my regular day off from both of my parish assignments. And in the compulsive Tobin way of doing things, they quickly assumed a highly disciplined routine.

After morning Mass, breakfast, and a few errands around the parish I'd arrive home about 11:00. We had a quick lunch, then Dad and I took off about 12:15 – every week. My mom didn't mind getting us out of the house. It was quiet time for her and she had her own routine, especially as she prepared for dinner. If, however, we weren't back by 4:00 there'd be lots of questions and worry. ("I thought something had happened!")

We usually went to one of two public nine hole courses in the North Hills section of Pittsburgh – Green Valley or Franklin Park. Green Valley was a narrow little course arranged in such a way that on just about every hole you'd be driving into other golfers walking toward you. "Suicide alley" it was sometimes called. We didn't go there very often.

Franklin Park was our home course. It was wide open and easy, not much more than a par three course. (Par was 32 I think.) No sand or water either. You could play that course, break 50 and feel pretty good about your game!

And Dad and I needed all the help we could get. If you had a picture next to the word "hackers" in the dictionary it'd be us. But we had really good excuses for our ineptitude. We didn't play very often after all. And I suspect that our clubs were deficient. My dad never did have a complete set, but just a starter set, and that with the brand name, "J.C. Higgins." (Never heard of it? It was the Sears-Roebuck brand name for sporting goods. Since Dad worked for Sears for almost 30 years, everything in our house came from Sears, except me I think.) My clubs weren't much better, though I had a complete set with a mainline name. I still have and use a "J.C. Higgins" putter, by the way.

Despite the lack of championship caliber play, our games were as competitive as anything you'd find on the PGA tour. Winning meant bragging rights for a week. And we gambled big time, 10 cents a hole. If someone happened to win all nine holes, which I did a few times, we'd round it off to a dollar, though it pained my dad to do so.

The best days at Franklin Park were in the middle of summer, when it was ninety – "hazy, hot and humid" the weather reports said – and sane people stayed home, out of the sun and away from golf courses. On those days there were no crowds, and thankfully no twosomes or foursomes on the first tee watching us drive, muffling their giggles at the topped shots dribbling down the hill.

It was really nice when we had the whole course to ourselves. Though by that time of the year the fairways were dry and dusty, and the greens brown, it didn't really matter. Undaunted we plodded up and down the hills of Franklin Park pulling our shaky golf carts (also from Sears) behind us. Life was good. I was with my dad and we were having fun.

I usually won our mini golf tournaments, and pocketed about 30 cents a week.

But not always. I remember at least one time that Dad beat me. I handed over the dime reluctantly and pouted. He was so proud and happy it made me happy, though I didn't admit it.

Then it was back home to repair to the front porch or back porch, whichever was in use that day, for a drink or two – gin and tonic for him, a martini or scotch for me – and some conversation between father and son while also describing our tournament to Mom. After dinner it was a couple more hours of relaxing, visiting with neighbors, tracking the Pirates game on the radio, and listening to Mom and Dad read the newspaper to each other. They did that a lot. Then for me it was back to the rectory. In those days priests seldom had "overnights." We always had to be at the church for Mass the next morning.

After my dad passed away one of the hardest things I had to do was dispose of his golf clubs, a hand-me-down gift to one of my young nephews I think. The clubs weren't worth much – a partial, old, worn set with that very funny name, "J.C. Higgins" – but they were priceless to me for the memories they inspired.

I don't play golf very much anymore – a tight schedule and even tighter back conspire to make it difficult. And maybe that's okay. Without my dad golf isn't nearly as much fun as it used to be, though the memories of our time together still make me happy.

CHAPTER 13

Things I Learned from Mom and Dad

Some very sad news stories involving neglected or abused children recently caught my attention but also reminded me how blessed I am to have had good parents, really good parents. Not only did my mom and dad provide for my basic care, protection and education, they also taught me some practical lessons that continue to serve me well.

For example, my parents taught me the value of punctuality.

For my dad especially, this was a very important human virtue. If we were going to church, setting out for a doctor's appointment or simply leaving for a family gathering, he wanted to be on time. I remember him saying, "I hate being late for anything. I'd rather be fifteen minutes early than five minutes late." And again, "Never keep someone waiting. Another person's time is just as valuable as yours."

I try hard to follow Dad's example of punctuality. I like to be on time and I don't like to keep people waiting. I also try to be patient with others who don't follow the same rules. Perhaps you know some people, as I do, who are habitually late, whose concept of time is just a little bit different. Nonetheless, when those situations do occur, Dad's instructions come quickly to mind.

My parents taught me the value of living a simple, uncluttered, and organized life.

In our home, discipline with time was complemented by discipline with things. We weren't collectors and we didn't accumulate junk. Our house was neat and organized, not cluttered. When we were finished using something it was put in its proper place. If we didn't need it anymore it was discarded, not dumped in the basement or garage. The appearance of our house changed very little from day to day, or even from year to year. There was a definite efficiency in our approach, a reassuring peacefulness in our routine. It seems that members of the Tobin family have inherited this trait. With the possible exception of my sister, I'm the worst offender. My desk is clean. My books are organized by topic and size. My shoes are arranged by color and date of purchase. My clocks, watches, and timers, all 35 of them, are synchronized. I admit it, I'm compulsive. But I like it that way. I don't understand how people can function otherwise!

From my parents I learned the joy of having good friends, lifelong friends.

My mom and dad had lots of friends they treasured throughout their lives. For years after our family moved from the East End of Pittsburgh to the North Hills, we returned to the old neighborhood at Christmastime to visit friends and "see their Christmas tree." Mom and Dad made an effort to stay in touch with old friends, visiting their homes or inviting them to ours to play cards, chat, share food and drink, and simply enjoy life.

Doesn't it seem to you that it's more difficult nowadays to maintain long friendships? Perhaps we're more mobile;

perhaps we're too busy. But when a friendship ends, through the natural course of events or some personal offense, we have the tendency to say, "better for having met; no worse for having parted." My parents taught me a different value: "A faithful friend is a sturdy shelter; he who finds one finds a treasure." (Sir 6:14)

Finally, from my parents I learned the importance of practical, everyday faith.

My parents weren't overly involved in the social activities or ministries of our Church. Of course in their day there weren't too many "ministries" other than helping with bingo, counting the collection, and cleaning the church. Nonetheless, faith in God was a given in our family, a way of life. We attended Mass every Sunday and holy day; we went to confession at least once a month; we put our envelopes in the basket; we respected our priests and nuns. At home we had devotional pictures and statues, said our prayers before meals, and learned the importance of doing good deeds for others. For Mom that included cookies and greeting cards; for Dad it meant helping family and neighbors whenever the need arose. For us, God wasn't a whirlwind who swept us away. He was the air we breathed everyday.

Perhaps it's from my parents' life example that I've learned, and have tried to preach, that if God is real, then faith is important. And if faith is authentic, it makes a difference in our lives everyday, not just on Sunday.

On Thanksgiving Day, I will again thank God that I had such wise and loving parents who taught me, by word and example, some of the good things in life. I hope you've had the same experience. If so, be grateful. It's a real gift!

CHAPTER 14

The View from the Back of the Ambulance

During my recent illness and hospitalization I had a couple of brand new experiences.

First, was the request by the physical therapist that I would try walking with a cane. The goal was to take some of the weight off my affected leg and allow me to move around a bit. I have to say it was a blow to my ego. I always thought that canes were for old people. (Careful – I know what you're thinking!) And as one who has used a much larger walking stick, a shepherd's staff, a crosier, for the last 14 years, walking with a cane was very different. It wasn't especially helpful for me this time around, but I suspect that before my days have ended I'll have the chance to try again.

The other, more compelling, first-time experience for me was riding in the back of an ambulance. Thank God I had never needed to be transported to a hospital in an ambulance before. And even this time, it wasn't on an emergency basis – but only because the pain and paralysis in my leg made it impossible for me to get into a car.

But the relatively brief journey from my residence in East Providence to the local Catholic hospital, Our Lady of Fatima, was memorable. I remember thinking, first of all, that perhaps this is how my last moments will be spent – on a stretcher, in the back of an ambulance, on the way to the emergency room.

And I was really struck by the view from the back of the ambulance, a view that one seldom has the opportunity to experience.

It was strange having the ambulance pull out of my driveway, leaving two friends, my dog and the Steeler banner receding in the background. It was strange heading to the hospital, not knowing what the next few hours or days would hold for me, completely abandoning the tight control I usually have over every detail of my life and schedule.

It was strange driving along familiar roads that I travel each day - the Wampanoag Trail, Route 195 and the streets of Providence - looking backwards at all the surroundings slipping away. It's a perspective one seldom has since we almost always look ahead when we're walking, running, riding, or driving. We usually face the direction we're going, not the places we've left behind.

If you think about it, the view from the back of the ambulance serves as a fitting metaphor for life, one that's especially relevant at this time of the year.

We've just ended one year and started a new one. I wonder if you've had the opportunity to look back and think about the experiences of the past year. Was it a good year or a bad one? Did you have good health or illness? Did you meet with some success in your professional life or suffer through embarrassing failures? Any new babies in your family last year? Lose any loved ones to eternal life? End up with a new job, a new home, or a new car? Any marriages or divorces among your friends? Take any great trips during the year or did you stay close to home? Did you grow in virtue or fall into sin? Did you move closer to God in 2006 or further way?

In short, what does 2006 look like now as you peer backwards and it begins to recede from view?

The same metaphorical look from the back window can be applied to your entire life, not just a year. Looking back, life passes quickly, doesn't it? I'm keenly aware that based on actuarial studies my life is about three-quarters over. Of course, it could end sooner, and that would be okay.

As the Psalmist reminds us:

"Seventy is the sum of our years, or eighty, if we are strong; Most of them are sorrow and toil; they pass quickly, we are all but gone." (Ps 90: 9-10)

That's it in a nutshell: the years pass quickly and we just drift away.

It's a good exercise, then, to look back and reflect upon your life, to think about the good and the bad, the positive and the negative, to assemble all the pieces of the puzzle so that a clear picture emerges. Everything you've experienced in life – what does it mean? Have you done what God has asked you to do? Have you fulfilled your purpose in life?

One final point. In riding in the back of the ambulance, it's impossible to see where you're going. You don't know what lies ahead on the road. You trust your journey to someone else, hoping they'll know the way and will get you to your destination in safety.

And so it is with the future. You really don't know what 2007 will hold for you, do you? You have no idea what will come your way.

Really, all you can do is work hard, take care of yourself, and try to do good things. Then place yourself in God's hands, confident that He knows the way and will get you to your final destination in safety.

CHAPTER 15

Peter, Paul and Mary

This is a story about Peter, Paul and Mary. No, not the great Apostles and beloved Mother of Jesus, but the other Peter, Paul and Mary – you know, the singing trio, the folk group. If you're under a certain age, let's say about thirty, you probably don't know much about Peter, Paul and Mary – known to their groupies as "PP&M." But if I mention songs like "Puff the Magic Dragon," "Blowin' in the Wind," "If I Had a Hammer," "Leaving on a Jet Plane," and "This Land is Your Land," perhaps you'll feel a little more comfortable!

Peter, Paul and Mary are first of all folk singers, but they're folk singers with a conscience. In the early days they fought against racism as they marched in Selma, Alabama and Washington, DC. They've railed against wars in Vietnam, El Salvador and Iraq. They've sung in support of the homeless, the hungry, laborers and immigrants. In their music they continue to challenge, and sometimes irritate, promoting a world view that is more peaceful, just, loving, and liberal.

My personal affection for Peter, Paul and Mary was rekindled recently when, through the courtesy of my nephew, Dan, I attended their concert in Lowell, Mass. Peter, Paul and Mary have been in the public spotlight now for forty-five years, and my affair with them goes back to almost the beginning.

When my family purchased a new "hi-fi system" in the early 1960s, one of the first long-playing, 33 rpm albums I bought was the two-record set, *Peter, Paul and Mary in Concert.* I still have it.

When I was named a bishop in 1992 I received a hand-written note from Mary Travers, congratulating me and encouraging me to keep the faith.

A few years ago they recorded a Christmas special for PBS television and I watch it, religiously, two or three times every holiday season.

I've attended at least five of their concerts spanning five decades.

The first was in Miami, perhaps in 1965-66, with my mom and dad during a seminary-approved version of spring break. It was a rainy, stormy night in Miami with terrible driving conditions but my mom and dad, God rest them, had obtained concert tickets to surprise me and they were determined to get me there.

I next remember seeing PP&M in concert in Pittsburgh, about 1968, when a group of seminarians, now in college, traveled from Loretto, PA, to Pittsburgh's famed Syria Mosque for the performance. A classmate's family owned a flower shop in Pittsburgh and had arranged to have flowers, daisies I think, sent to Mary backstage. We actually met her after the concert and when he brazenly asked for a kiss on the cheek she turned him down and warned that he was falling into sin!

The next concert I attended, again in Pittsburgh, about twenty years later, was probably the most memorable. A great performance, as always, but during the concert while

Peter, Paul and Mary were on stage singing about peace, love and joy, a violent fight broke out in the audience in the section right behind us. I'll never forget the incongruity of the moment.

Just two years ago I attended an outdoor summer concert in Pittsburgh with several young friends. The freight trains traveling in and out of Pittsburgh passed right behind the concert venue and disrupted the music several times. PP&M were obviously annoyed but compensated very nicely by spontaneously launching into their song "Freight Train, Freight Train" every time a train passed by.

And then there was the concert last month in Lowell. Obviously the audience has aged. You can tell that's the case when the line at the handicapped entrance is longer than the other lines. Lots of wheelchairs, canes, gray hair, no hair, and flowered nylon shirts. Nephew Dan was nice enough to remind me that it might be the last time I'd ever see Peter, Paul and Mary in concert – not because of their condition, but because of mine. (I've written him out of my will!)

Peter, Paul and Mary have changed too, of course. Mary has just survived a courageous battle with cancer. She's lost a lot of weight and some of her vocal range. Paul forgot some lyrics and Peter stumbled around the stage a little bit, looking for but never finding his capo. (Ask your closest guitar player.)

It didn't really matter. It was easy to overlook the mistakes and imperfections and even the left-leaning political commentary. The concert was great and the crowd loved it. We sang along to the familiar tunes, with or without prompting from the stage. The affection for the trio was real, perhaps because we realized that indeed "*the times they are a changin.*" When as their finale PP&M sang "This Land is Your Land" the Lowell Memorial Auditorium fairly rocked – okay, at least as much as several thousand golden-agers can rock anything beyond a chair.

There are lots of problems in the world today, in our Church and community too. But without a doubt, everything seems just a little better, a little brighter, when you sing along with Peter, Paul and Mary.

Okay, all together now: *"Puff the Magic Dragon, lived by the sea . . ."*

CHAPTER 16

Sports: The Toy Department of Human Life

The insightful description of sports inscribed above is attributed to the late, great American sports journalist Howard Cosell. It also serves as a perfect introduction to this column about the virtues and vices of the world of sports.

Without a doubt, we've entered one of the best times of the year for sports fans. The playoffs and World Series are on the doorstep; the football season, on professional, college, and high school levels, has begun; hockey and basketball fans don't have much longer to wait until their interminable seasons begin; and even the waning golf season has a few lingering events before the boys pack up their clubs and go home for the winter.

It can be an intense time of the year, especially for a black and gold Pittsburgh fan living in the midst of red, white, and blue New England. I was reminded of that cruel reality a few weeks ago.

On a sparkling late-summer Friday morning, I stopped at a local bank that was celebrating, apparently, New England sports day. The office was filled with red, white, and blue streamers and balloons. Large posters of New England sports heroes adorned the walls. The employees were wearing T-shirts and sweatshirts carrying names like Brady and Bruschi, Ortiz and Matsuzaka.

Since I was on my way to the office, I was wearing my clerical collar. One local citizen, a couple of places ahead of me in line, turned around, spotted me and said, "Hey, aren't you that Steeler fan?" Obviously he was less concerned about my state in life than my sports allegiance.

The bank grew silent, customers and employees dropped their work, watching and waiting for my response. (I was reminded of the scene in the Passion narrative when bystanders said to St. Peter: "Aren't you one of that man's followers?")

Showing more courage than Peter, though, I put on my best "and what do you want to make of it?" attitude and responded in a loud, defiant voice, "Yes, I am, and if I knew this party was going on today I would have worn my Steeler sweatshirt."

I thought I'd need police protection!

Again a few days later, my Steeler heart was broken when I read the front page of the sports section of *The Providence Journal* to learn about the local Barrington Carmelite Nuns' unabashed loyalty to the New England Patriots and how they were wined and dined in Foxboro by Bob Kraft, owner of the Patriots. The Sisters said they'd be praying for the Patriots this season. I immediately ran to the Code of Canon Law to see if the Sisters could be excommunicated for such blasphemy. No such luck. Nonetheless, I take this opportunity to remind the sisters who their landlord is!

Ah, sports can be so much fun. Of course if sports are an accurate reflection of the human condition, as many commentators have suggested, there is often a dark side, too.

We've been reminded of the faults and failures of some of our sports heroes. There's Barry Bond's steroid-enhanced chase of the home-run record. With complete revulsion, we followed the reports of quarterback Michael Vick's involvement in the disgusting world of dog fighting. And even the previously untarnished Tom Brady disappointed some of his fans when the sordid details of his extramarital liaisons were revealed. (Tom and Bridget receive high marks, though, at least in my book, for bringing their baby to birth, when many other couples facing similar circumstances would have chosen a far less noble option for their unborn child!)

Then there was a report that former Steeler running-back Jerome Bettis, the "Bus," admitted to faking an injury towards the end of his playing career. I don't believe it, though. Steelers don't do things like that!

It's undeniable that sports can bring out the negative tendencies in human nature. The fun and excitement of athletic competition is often undermined by the unhealthy interference of parents, the unruly behavior of fans, attacks on officials, excessive drinking, irresponsible gambling, foul language, and the increase of domestic abuse reported each year on Super Bowl Sunday.

While sports are wonderful, they have to be kept in perspective. This is a particular challenge in our schools, where athletic accomplishments sometimes rule the roost and completely overshadow academic achievement and other important school activities.

For the most part, however, athletic competition on both an amateur and professional level is positive and healthy. It should be applauded and supported. Sports develop positive human and Christian virtues and teach valuable lessons. They promote healthy bodies, minds, and spirits.

Sports should be fun – the "toy department of human life," as Howard Cosell put it. But they have to take a proportionate place among other important realities of life. The legendary basketball coach John Wooden insisted: "What you are as a person is far more important than what you are as a basketball player."

CHAPTER 17

A Son of the Beach

Once again this year my summer vacation took me to a beach. Without a doubt it's my favorite kind of vacation. No historic churches, famous museums, or amusement parks for me. No, sir. While on vacation I look for nothing more than sun, sand, and surf. It's on the beach that I find relaxation, renewal, and peace. I guess it's true, as some have suggested, that I really am a "son of the beach!"

Beyond the obvious aesthetic benefits, however, time on the beach also provides some important spiritual lessons, lessons about God, lessons about our pilgrimage in life.

First, the beach, and the water that surrounds it, has a timeless quality. It serves as an icon of infinity.

As I walked on the shoreline of the Gulf of Mexico I realized that those same waves have been washing up upon the same shore for hundreds, thousands, perhaps millions of years: long before the events of September 11th; long before the foundation of our country and the discovery of New World; long before the birth of Christ and the Roman, Greek and Egyptian Empires; and long before human footprints sullied the sands of any beach anywhere.

And the abundance of it all! How many waves soak into the sand each day? How many gallons of water in the sea? How many grains of sand on the beach?

If we're attentive to the signs, the beach speaks to us of the infinity and perfection of God and the dignity of each human person. Despite the fact that each of us is but one small speck of sand in the universe, a fleeting moment in the long history of the world, we possess infinite value in the sight of God. Here we find an echo of Psalm 8: "O, Lord our God, when I see the heavens, the work of your hands, the moon and the stars which you arranged, what is man that you should keep him in mind, mortal man that you care for him? And yet you have made him little less than a god; with glory and honor you crowned him."

Time on the beach also creates a healthy perspective on the trials and tribulations of life.

During my week in Florida this year, on two consecutive evenings I watched fierce thunderstorms quickly develop, sweep over the shoreline, and dramatically change the entire panorama. Just a few minutes earlier the sky was blue, the sun was bright, the surf was gentle and inviting. But then the storm arrived, accompanied by dark and ominous skies, violent and dangerous lightning, winds strong enough to move porch furniture, drenching rain that blew sideways and waves that pounded the shoreline with remarkable force.

Then, as quickly as it began, the storm was over and life on the beach became tranquil once again.

Isn't our life like that too? We roll along, rather peacefully, without major problems, enjoying, even taking for granted, the gifts and blessings the Lord has given us. But then a storm develops – a family crisis, a serious health problem, the death of a loved one, the loss of a job – and the peace and tranquility we had enjoyed is completely obliterated, seemingly never to return again.

In the difficult personal moments we inevitably encounter, we need to believe that the present storm will pass and that someday, in God's Providence, our lives will be secure and peaceful again.

Finally, I find that time on the beach naturally leads us to the horizon and that's a very good thing to happen.

As I sat on the balcony of my third-floor apartment during the day, I often looked out to sea as far I could, wondering how far I could travel before finding another shore, wondering exactly what was on the other side. And in the darkness of the night, from the same perch, I could see the lights of distant ships, moving silently to some destination I could not know, but only imagine.

Too often we get so caught up in the present moment, in the circumstances and details of everyday life, that we forget about the future. Do you ever take time to gaze at the horizon of your own life? Do you ever speculate on what the future holds for you and your loved ones? Do you think about heaven and what it must be like?

Once in awhile, as you walk along the shoreline of life, it's good and healthy to lift your eyes to the horizon, joyfully embrace the future and renew your confidence in God who will surely lead you to a safe and peaceful harbor.

CHAPTER 18

Ashley's World

You know what it is to be a child? It is to be something very different from the man of today. It is to have a spirit yet streaming from the waters of baptism,' it is to believe in love, to believe in loveliness, to believe in belief; it is to be so little that the elves can reach to whisper in your ear,' it is to turn pumpkins into coaches, and mice into horses, lowness into loftiness, and nothing into everything, for each child has its fairy godmother in its soul. It is to live in a nutshell and count yourself the king of infinite space,' to see a world in a grain of sand and a heaven in a wildflower,' to hold infinity in the palm of your hand, and eternity in an hour. (Francis Thompson)

A few weeks ago it was my grand privilege to baptize Ashley Margaret, the beautiful daughter and third child of my friends Debbie and Joe. Ashley was born on December 26th, a welcome Christmas gift for her mom and dad, her siblings Michael and Amber, and a very excited and loving extended family.

Although I don't baptize infants as often as I used to, it's an invitation I accept whenever I can. Baptism is a very special moment in the life of the child, the family, and the Church, and indeed a privilege for anyone who administers the sacrament.

On such occasions I enjoy the opportunity of holding the newborn child of God. It provides a remarkably peaceful and reflective moment. One rule, however, is always observed -baby is quickly returned to the closest parent the moment the little bundle of joy gets restless or cranky, or is otherwise in need of servicing!

On the afternoon of Ashley's Baptism, I held her a couple of times -once during the family photo session and then again during lunch while Mom was eating. Ashley was rather oblivious to all the excitement around her and fell asleep quickly in my arms.

Before Ashley drifted off, however, I couldn't help but look into her eyes and wonder exactly what she was seeing, hearing, and thinking at that moment. I also began some personal musings that continued for me on the way home and throughout the day. I thought about the kind of world Ashley had entered. And I wondered what that world would be like for Ashley in the future, as an active teenager in 15 years or so, and when she is a mature adult in 25, 30 or 40 years.

I wonder...will Ashley's world continue to be a place of violence and war where guns and bombs settle international disputes, or will the world see an increase of justice and peace so that disputes are resolved by reasonable men (and women) through discussion and compromise?

In Ashley's world will there still be so much violence and fear that it's impossible to travel without the burden of oppressive security, or will she be able to move about the nation and around the world in relative comfort and peace?

Will the people of Ashley's world continue to solve their problems by the needless taking of human life in abortion, euthanasia, capital punishment, street crime, and terrorism, or will civilized people finally have learned to respect human life as the premier gift of God, protecting especially their weakest and most vulnerable neighbors?

In Ashley's world, will science be abused to create new weapons of mass destruction, manipulate nature, and clone human beings, or will it be used in a positive way to cure disease, end famine, and eliminate poverty from the face of the earth?

Will Ashley grow up in a cold electronic world overrun by computers, cell phones, video cameras, and inventions yet to be imagined, or will technology serve people, enabling them to relax, communicate effectively, and enjoy the blessings of friendship?

And what about the entertainment in Ashley's world? Will the culture of the time be known for superficial, vulgar characters like Jerry Springer, Eminem, and the Osbourne's, or by great and enduring artists like Shakespeare, Michelangelo, and Mozart?

In Ashley's world will people still be numbered and divided by lines of race, religion, and national heritage, or will they recognize how much they share, how much they have in common as children of God?

Will Ashley grow up in a world that minimizes the family, ridicules traditional values, and celebrates every deviant lifestyle in the name of diversity, or in a world that supports the institution of marriage, affirms family life, and welcomes children as essential ingredients of God's plan for the perfection of mankind?

Will Ashley's world have completely exhausted the natural resources of the earth and fouled the water, air, and food beyond use, or will mankind have learned to conserve its resources and protect the planet for the use of future generations?

Wow...so many questions, so few answers. If only we had a crystal ball to tell us of the future, we could give Ashley at least a hint of what awaits her in the years to come. But of course that's not possible, and it's just as well, I'm sure.

Now, by nature I'm an optimist. I greet each day with, "Good morning, God," and not "Good God, morning." I usually see the glass half full, not half empty. I tend to give people the benefit of the doubt and not jump on their failures. And if anything, I'm naive, not cynical. Nonetheless, I must confess to some apprehension about the quality of Ashley's world. Perhaps I'm concerned about the evident lack of spiritual, moral, and human progress. Maybe I'm so focused on the challenges and problems of today, I can't begin to imagine tomorrow's solutions.

In the end, however, I know my anxiety's unfounded. I have to trust God's presence, power, and love, His infallible plan for the redemption of the world. Should I be tempted to do otherwise, I need only listen again to His stinging reproof of Job during his time of doubt:

"Who is this that obscures divine plans with words of ignorance? Gird up your loins now, like a man; I will question you, and you tell me the answers! Where were you when I founded the earth? Tell me, if you have understanding. And who shut within doors the sea, when it burst forth from the womb? Have you ever in your lifetime commanded the morning and shown the dawn its place? Have you comprehended the breadth of the earth? Tell me, if you know all: Which is the way to the dwelling place of light, and where is the abode of darkness? You know, because you were born before them, and the number of your years is great!" (Cf Job 38)

So, Ashley, here's to you, kid, and to you, Michael and Amber, and to all your peers. We pray that God will be with you always, that He will bless you abundantly, and that the world you inherit will be far better than anything we can imagine today!

CHAPTER 19

My Little Black Book

There is an appointed time for everything, and a time for every affair under the heavens. A time to be born, and a time to die. (Eccl 3:1-2)

This well-known passage from the Book of Ecclesiastes emphasizes the many diverse experiences that are part of the human journey.

I encountered the same thing recently when I began rewriting my personal address book, my little black book. (Actually it was green but "My Little Black Book" makes for a better title.) In an age when many people have their address books on their computer, the fact that I have an address book in hard copy makes me a dinosaur, I guess. Nonetheless, I do and once in a while it needs to be updated.

My little black book had 116 entries involving about 182 people. It had been about ten years, I think, since I rewrote the entire book, and I was stunned by the number of changes that have occurred in the lives of family members, friends, and acquaintances during those years.

Fifteen people have died, including my mom, my brother, and an aunt. May they rest in peace.

Some experienced serious illness in recent years. Some have recovered, some are suffering still.

Lots of people have moved, sometimes more than once, usually in search of bigger homes, (although some of the older folks have downsized) or new and better jobs.

My family and friends are not immune to social trends, and sadly there have been far too many separations and divorces, disrupting the lives of families and children, resulting in the loss of contact with extended family members whom I had come to know and love.

The changes in my little black book reflected lots of good news, too. There have been beautiful weddings, the birth of precious new children, families growing and prospering, Baptisms, Confirmations and graduations, new homes, new schools, and new professions.

I'm surprised at the number of people I was in contact with ten years ago who have disappeared from my life, usually not through animosity or anger, but more often as a consequence of people moving or becoming busy, then losing regular contact and shared experiences. One author observed that most relationships, short of marriage, are destined to end through natural causes, and when they do, we should be able to say simply, peacefully, "Better for having met, no worse for having parted." It seems like a cold, heartless saying, but in reviewing my address book, I think it's true.

On the other hand, in establishing my new address book, I'm pleased by the number of people I've met in recent years, the new friends and acquaintances who have become part of my life's story.

"There is an appointed time for everything, and a time for

every affair under the heavens."

You may or may not have a little black book, but think of all the changes you've experienced in your own life over the last ten years. Maybe members of your family and friends have died or struggled with serious illness. Perhaps you've gotten engaged or married, or suffered a painful separation and divorce. Maybe you've moved to a new home or taken a new job. Perhaps you've lost contact with some really close friends or met that one very special person destined to be your best friend, your confidant, your lover.

Without a doubt, life is filled with unpredictable change, and for that reason it's nearly impossible to foretell the future, the silly claims of psychics notwithstanding. Who knows where you'll be or what you'll be doing ten years from now, or next year – or even tomorrow for that matter.

There are three things, however, I can predict of the future with absolute certainty.

First, it will be a mixture of good and bad, success and failure, victory and defeat, health and illness, life and death. I can predict that with certainty because such experiences are part of life every year, every day.

Second, the future will be as good or as bad as you choose to make it. The good and the bad, the successes and failures, the moments of life and death – these events are the natural resources, the raw materials God places into your hands. What you do with them, and how you respond, is up to you.

Finally, I predict that regardless of what you encounter in the future, God will be with you. That's one of the primary tenets of our Christian Faith, isn't it? We believe in Emmanuel, "God with us." And we find courage in the words of Jesus, "Behold, I am with you always, until the end of the age." (Mt 28:20)

The point is this: In the midst of all the changes that come our way, our faith in God is the rock-solid foundation on which we build our lives, the harbor that gives us safe shelter from the stormy seas we are bound to traverse in our voyage of life.

CHAPTER 20

Let's Check the Baggage

Having had several opportunities to travel this summer, I've witnessed a growing and irritating trend – the increasing amount of "stuff" that passengers take with them onto the planes.

The rules for carry-on bags are clear enough – one small suitcase (small enough for the overhead bin or the place under the seat in front of you) and one small personal item, such as a purse or briefcase. Apparently lots of folks have decided the rules don't apply to them, and they routinely board the planes with supersized suitcases, doubled-over garment bags, shopping bags filled with souvenirs, purses, computers, and in the winter, bulky, heavy coats rolled and stuffed into the compartments. No wonder it takes forever to board the plane and get people situated.

But the boarding process is made even more perilous these days because passengers have lots of other things to manage. How often I've watched individuals making their perilous journey down the crowded aisle of the plane (with all of the above-mentioned items) while talking on their cell phones, ("I just got on the plane -I'll call you when

I get to my seat.") carrying a box of pizza, squeezing a newspaper under their arm and, of course, clutching the now forbidden bottle of water.

Without a doubt, we travel with too much baggage. But the airport experience just typifies our daily life, doesn't it? We all have too much stuff! I'm as guilty as the next guy! Even though I never hesitate to throw things away, and despite the fact that I'm disciplined and organized (some would say compulsive), with a neat, uncluttered home and desk, I have too much stuff.

I realized that again on the Fourth of July when I spent a quiet, personal day at home finally completing the process of unpacking the boxes that had come with me from Ohio. Most of the unpacking had taken place right after I moved. But there were still three or four boxes of things I hadn't touched for over a year. As I unloaded the boxes and arranged everything on the basement floor, I wondered out loud, "Why did I bring all of this stuff with me?"

There were pictures, picture frames, picture cubes, and photo albums. There were candles, candle holders, statues, crucifixes, icons, religious pictures, prayer books, and holy water bottles. There were mementos from my studies in Rome, my Priesthood Ordination, parish assignments, and my Episcopal Ordination and Installation in Youngstown. There were souvenirs from concerts, ball games, family gatherings, and church events. There were paper weights, letter openers, pen and pencil sets, leather folders, and clocks that no longer worked. And there was that shoebox that my dad had packed for me about 30 years ago, a little emergency kit for the trunk of my car – with a flashlight, paper and pencil (to write down information in case of an accident), a fluorescent safety flag, tools to make repairs to the car, and few rags to wipe the grease from my hands.

I have too much stuff.

I don't have as many clothes as most people, I suspect, but I have far more than I need. Just for the heck of it, I did a little survey and found that I own 103 shirts. Shirts of all kinds – black shirts, white shirts, long-sleeved and short-sleeved shirts, sport shirts, flannel shirts, and T-shirts. Why do I need 103 shirts? I only wear one at a time. The rest of my wardrobe is similarly overstocked, despite the fact that I just gave away a bunch of clothes.

I have too much stuff.

We all have too much stuff – in our daily lives and, perhaps, in our personal lives as well.

It seems to me that the material baggage we accumulate is sometimes matched by the emotional baggage we carry around with us, the ghosts from the past – the personal failures, the sorrows, the disappointments, the regrets, the anger, the bitterness, the pain – and lots of other things that would be better left behind.

And what about the baggage that clutters our spiritual lives? The sins of the past and present; the temptations with which we flirt; the evil thoughts, words, and deeds; the bad habits and destructive relationships? Once in awhile our spiritual home needs a good housecleaning too!

In the Gospel, when Jesus commissioned the Disciples to go forth and proclaim the Kingdom, He instructed them to travel lightly. On one hand it was an invitation to depend on God alone, to trust in His Providence. But it was also a practical reminder that too much stuff can weigh us down and hold us back.

Next time you travel through an airport, pay attention to the baggage that people carry with them. And then take a personal inventory. Can your life be simplified? Do you have too much stuff? Are there material, emotional, or spiritual things you need to throw away?

Let's check the baggage. Let's travel lightly and move forward, enjoying the freedom we have as children of God.

Faith Through the Seasons

CHAPTER 21

The Chrism Mass: Renewing Priestly Service

Without a doubt, Holy Week marks the high point of the liturgical year. It's a very significant time for every Catholic, as we follow Jesus with a lively faith and strive to share once again in the fullness of the Paschal Mystery. As the *Preface for the Passion of the Lord* reminds us: "The days of His life-giving death and glorious Resurrection are approaching. This is the hour when Christ triumphed over Satan's pride, the time when we celebrate the great event of our redemption."

But if Holy Week is special for all God's People, it has particular meaning for our priests, and one of the celebrations that highlights that truth is the annual Chrism Mass.

The Chrism Mass is always celebrated during Holy Week. At this beautiful and rich liturgy, the holy oils that are used for the sacraments throughout the year are blessed and then distributed to our parishes. Additionally, as the *Roman Missal* says, "This Mass, which the bishop concelebrates with his presbyterium manifests the communion of the priests with their bishop . . . To show the unity of the presbyterium, the priests who concelebrate with the bishop should come from different parts of the diocese."

The Chrism Mass, renewed in recent years, has become a vibrant event in many dioceses. In Providence too, it is a very special part of our liturgical life, bringing together most of the priests and many of the faithful of our diocesan Church. It's wonderful to see so many of our priests together at the same time and their presence is a visible manifestation of the unity they have with their bishop and, just as importantly, with one another.

One feature of the Chrism Mass is the renewal of commitment to priestly service. The bishop asks the priests, gathered in the cathedral where most of them were ordained, and in the presence of God's People: "Are you ready to renew your own dedication to Christ as priests of the new covenant? Are you resolved to unite yourselves more closely to Christ and try to become more like him? Are you resolved to be faithful ministers of the mysteries of God? Are you resolved to imitate Jesus Christ, the head and shepherd of the Church?" To each of these questions, the priests respond: "I am."

As the ceremony of renewal continues the bishop asks the faithful to pray for their priests, "to help them be faithful ministers of Christ the High Priest." The bishop also asks the people to pray for him as well, "that despite my own unworthiness, I may faithfully fulfill the office of apostle which Jesus Christ has entrusted to me."

As a bishop leading the renewal of priestly commitment for eleven years now in two dioceses, I sense that this moment is much more than just a formal ritual for our priests. The recommitment is personal, sincere, and moving. It's clear that our priests are grateful for their vocation, mindful of the importance of their work, and are eager to renew their commitment to serve Christ and His Church.

On the first Holy Thursday, Jesus instituted the ministerial priesthood at the Last Supper. But the priesthood never exists in the abstract. Around the table in the Upper Room it was made flesh in the Apostles gathered with the Lord. And throughout the history of the Church it has taken form in countless other men, imperfect individuals with failings and foibles. Priests know, better than anyone else, that they are but "earthen vessels, that the surpassing power may be of God and not from us." (2 Cor 4:7)

Since arriving in the Diocese of Providence I've been genuinely impressed by the priests of the diocese. They are sincere, talented, and hardworking; they serve generously without complaining. Their service spans several generations. We have an encouraging number of dedicated young priests, still learning, but intelligent and multitalented, confident in their identity and clearly in love with the Lord. We have lots of priests who are middle-aged, growing in grace and wisdom, often facing serious challenges in their daily ministry, but still anxious to do the work of the Lord. And we have a good number of "senior priests," now retired from active administration but, in many cases still active ministers of the Lord, helping out here and there, and always supporting us by their prayers and good example.

On this occasion I would like to again sincerely thank the priests of the Providence Diocese for their personal kindness to me, their support of my ministry, and for all they do as priests of the Lord Jesus Christ.

I also encourage you, dear readers, to take a moment during Holy Week to express a word of gratitude to your priests. Perhaps you can drop them a note or thank them in person. But don't take your priests for granted. Help them, support them, and pray for them, everyday!

Please remember, too, those priests who have experienced difficulties in their lives: those who struggle with illness or other personal problems; those who through human weakness have failed in their ministry and on occasion even hurt their people; and those, who for a variety of reasons have left the ministry and moved on to another chapter in their life.

As the bishop concludes the renewal of commitment to priestly service at the Chrism Mass he says to the assembly, "May the Lord in his love keep you close to him always, and may he bring all of us, his priests and people, to eternal life." That's a fervent hope and a good prayer for all of us during the week we call "holy."

CHAPTER 22

Breaking News:
The Tomb of Jesus is Empty!

Depending on your point of view, it's either the most significant archeological find in history, with enormous theological consequences, or just another fraudulent publicity stunt aimed at promoting a silly television program. I vote for the latter.

The story in question, of course, is the announcement by filmmakers and researchers that they've discovered two ancient burial boxes containing the bones of Jesus and His family. Most legitimate scholars have completely discredited the scam. An archaeologist named Amos Kloner, the first to examine the burial site, said that the idea fails to meet any professional standards. "The claim that the burial site has been found is not based on any proof, and is only an attempt to sell," said Kloner. And Stephen Pfann, a renowned biblical scholar in Jerusalem, said that the film's hypothesis holds little weight. Nonetheless, the announcement that the body of Jesus has been discovered has generated a good deal of public curiosity.

The President of the Catholic League, Bill Donohue, summarized the situation very nicely. He says that James

Cameron, the director of the film, (who also directed the movie "Titantic"), has produced a "titanic fraud."

More troublesome to me than the secular publicity surrounding the "discovery," however, is the bizarre statement by a Catholic theologian at a prominent Catholic university that even if the body of Jesus was discovered, it wouldn't shake his faith. What? If he doesn't believe in the Resurrection, then what does he believe, and why? (I also worry about what he's teaching in the classroom!)

If it's true, that the body of Jesus was found in a Jerusalem suburb, then the Christian Faith is over. As St. Paul wrote, "And if Christ has not been raised, then empty (too) is our preaching; empty, too, your faith." (I Cor 15:14) That's pretty clear, isn't it?

And think of the personal consequences if Jesus was not raised from the dead.

If Jesus was not raised from the dead, then all of our Christian and Catholic beliefs and practices are suspect.

If Jesus was not raised from the dead, the Church is not the Body of Christ, enlivened and guided by the Holy Spirit. It's simply another social club and its work is built on a fraudulent foundation.

If Jesus was not raised from the dead, all of our loved ones who have passed away are simply gone and buried, with no hope of resurrection; we'll never see them again. And we have no hope of eternal life either.

And in very personal terms, if Jesus was not raised from the dead, my years of study and work are in vain. My sacrifices, promises, and commitments are for naught. I might as well pack it up, move on, get married, raise a family, and try to live a good, quiet, and productive life.

But in fact, I've bet my whole life on the fact that Jesus was raised from the dead and that He is the Lord and Savior of the world. If the filmmakers who have caused this fuss have produced any good, it's the opportunity for us to review our belief in the Lord's Resurrection and all that it means for us. It's a good exercise, especially during this Season of Lent.

The *Catechism of the Catholic Church* says the following: "The Resurrection above all constitutes the confirmation of all Christ's works and teachings . . . Christ's Resurrection is the fulfillment of the promises both of the Old Testament and of Jesus Himself . . . The truth of Jesus' divinity is confirmed by His Resurrection . . . Christ's Resurrection – and the Risen Christ Himself – is the principle and source of our future resurrection." (#651-655)

It's true, and one of the great ironies of history, that no one actually saw Christ rise from the dead. But, as the *Catechism* insists, "The mystery of Christ's Resurrection is a real event, with manifestations that were historically verified, as the New Testament bears witness." (#639) As you know, the classic proofs of the bodily Resurrection of Christ are the empty tomb and the many appearances of Christ after the Resurrection. And it's indisputable that something very dramatic happened to change the life of the Disciples – from weak, timid, frightened men, to courageous witnesses and preachers, willing to leave everything behind, travel the world, and sacrifice their lives for their convictions.

So, dear readers, the choice is yours. If you believe that after two-thousand years some movie producers and directors have really found the body of Jesus in an obscure tomb in the outskirts of Jerusalem, then don't go to Church this Sunday, Easter Sunday, or ever again.

If, however, you believe the core Christian doctrine that Christ was raised from the dead, you should go to Church this Sunday, Easter Sunday, and every other Sunday. Like the first Disciples your life should be transformed by the reality of Christ's Resurrection. And you should live your life in such a way that the world comes to believe that Jesus is Lord!

CHAPTER 23

"Back to School" Just Isn't the Same

The first thing I do with my Sunday paper is to sort through it and discard the ads that serve only to annoy me. In the process of doing so recently, one of the inserts caught my attention. It read, "Don't miss out on cool phones for back to school." "What?" I asked out loud. "Since when is a cell phone a 'back to school' necessity?" After all, I mused, I went through 12 years of grade school and high school and never once had to make a phone call from a classroom, hallway, or parking lot.

With my interest now piqued, however, I checked out a few other ads that had already been set aside. One offered to save me $200 on a 2.8GHz notebook computer, "the latest essential for back to school work and fun." Wouldn't help me get back to school – I wouldn't know a GHz if it smacked me in the head!

A third page of school supplies pictured a variety of Texas Instruments TI-83 plus graphing calculators with 192 KB of memory. "And don't forget your graphing calculator case," the ad reminded me, apparently concerned that my memory is nowhere near 192 KB.

It's clear that going back to school just isn't the same as it used to be.

Despite my shortage of KBs, I do recall the excitement of buying fresh supplies guaranteed to make the new school year a grand success. There really was something exhilarating and hopeful about buying brand new, clean, never-touched-by-human-hands pencils, pens, rulers, and notebooks (the kind with paper).

One of the highlights of my back-to-school shopping was the purchase of a new, blue, cloth-covered, three-ringed binder – with a sturdy metal clip on the inside cover and five plastic tabs to separate distinct subjects. I bonded with that binder and used it well into high school I think. We experienced only a minor crisis in the Tobin household when I mistakenly purchased notebook paper with just two holes that obviously wouldn't fit the three-ringed binder. (My mom and dad, never comfortable wasting things, used that paper for household notes for many years.)

And who can forget the satisfaction of buying a brand new set of crayons at the beginning of the school year? My favorite was a box of 64 crayons, including some colors I never heard of and was afraid to use, arranged in several tiers for easy access. The real kicker – the box had a built-in pencil sharpener – cutting-edge technology for our day.

My elementary school, St. Teresa School in Perrysville, wasn't exempt from the incursion of prehistoric technology either.

I clearly remember the excitement of that September day in the late 1950s when we returned to school to find that our *black* blackboards had been replaced by *green* blackboards for the purpose, we were told, of reducing glare and saving our eyesight. That, right there, was enough to convince me of the value of technology!

And remember that gizmo, made of a wooden handle and five metal "fingers" that could hold five pieces of chalk simultaneously? It was designed to draw five parallel lines on the board – the new green blackboard – all at once, lines that were used for penmanship drills and music lessons.

And then there was the new electric eraser-cleaner, the mighty little vacuum used to suck chalk dust from the erasers that had erased the parallel lines that had been drawn on the board – the new green blackboard. We used to fight for the privilege of using the eraser-cleaning machine after school, for it was a lot easier and more fun than banging the erasers on the sidewalk and being overcome by a wave of chalk dust.

Oh well, since I remember with such fondness the technological advances that changed our schools in the 1950s I guess I have to accept the changes of this new millennium too, for without a doubt the rising tide of technology is as relentless in our schools as in society.

I just hope that the triumph of technology isn't just another pyrrhic victory of style over substance.

I hope that our kids still learn the basic ingredients of a good education – reading, writing and 'rithmetic.

And in our Catholic schools, I pray that our students know as much about Commandments as computers, are as comfortable in sacred space as cyberspace. If not, we might as well delete the whole darned thing!

Can you hear me now?

CHAPTER 24

Halloween Isn't So Scary

By now you've probably noticed that the stores are stocked with Christmas items – cards, decorations, trees, and gifts – a sure sign that Halloween is just around the corner! Of course the Halloween stuff has been on the counters since Labor Day so we should be well-prepared for our annual foray into the nether world.

I've read that Halloween is the second biggest commercial holiday of the year, right after Christmas, and it's certainly become a huge party day, for children, teens, and adults alike. And with each year comes the debate whether Halloween is Christian or pagan, good or evil. The Diocese of Providence isn't immune from the controversy.

For several years now during the Halloween season one of our diocesan youth centers has sponsored a "Haunted Labyrinth." It's intended to be a fun-filled activity for families and young people, as well as a fundraiser for youth ministry projects. I'm told, however, that each year some folks have expressed their sincere concern over the propriety of the activity. This year is no exception.

A few weeks ago I received a letter about the "Haunted Labyrinth" from a member of the diocese expressing his dismay that we would sponsor such a nefarious project. He says: "I feel that the Haunted Labyrinth can in effect cause scandal and confusion to many young Catholics, who rather, should be receiving formation that will allow them to know, love, and serve God . . . Our Catholic youth should be encouraged to imitate the saints rather than demons, witches, and warlocks. There must be a better way to raise funds in which our diocese can also receive God's blessing."

The writer raises some good points. Our young people certainly should be exposed to sound catechesis that teaches us to love and to serve the Lord; we should look to the saints as our heroes and role models; and the Church does need to be vigilant about the sources of its income.

In this context it might be helpful to mention the history of Halloween. Where did it come from and how did it evolve into its current form?

For the ancient Celtic tribes, November 1 marked the beginning of a new year and the coming of winter. The night before the New Year they celebrated the festival of *Samhain*, the Lord of the Dead. During this festival the people wore masks and lit bonfires to scare away the evil spirits that roamed the earth that night.

When the Romans conquered the Celts, they added a few of their own touches to the pagan festival, introducing some customs we'd be familiar with today, such as drinking apple cider and bobbing for apples. And finally in 835 Pope Gregory IV moved the Feast of the Martyrs (later All Saints) to November 1. The night before All Saints Day became known as All Hallows Eve, eventually shortened to Halloween.

But what about our current observance?

Well, without a doubt, Halloween has a dark and disturbing side. Each year we hear about dangerous activities that accompany the day. Cable channels are filled with

scary, violent films. Parents have to monitor the neighborhoods their children visit and then inspect the candy and
cookies for foreign objects or poison. And we're regularly
warned to protect our puppies and kittens lest some really
sick individuals steal them for animal sacrifice or demonic
activities.

But I think for most people, Halloween is more pleas-
ant and positive than that.

As a kid growing up in Pittsburgh, my experience of
Halloween was fun, not dangerous. It had everything to
do with candy, and nothing to do with Satan. I remember walking though our Laurel Gardens neighborhood in
an inexpensive costume my mom had purchased for a few
bucks, and I personally knew all of the streets and most of
the neighbors. (You see, at night I was the scary ghost or
skeleton, but by day I was the friendly and reliable paper-
boy.) I carried a brown paper shopping bag, going door
to door with a couple of friends, hurrying to the houses
distributing the best candy bars. On warm evenings it got
really hot and sweaty in that costume and if it rained it
was even worse since both my costume and the paper bag
quickly dissolved. More than once I lost a boatload of
candy on Eighth Avenue just before I got home. But there
were no destructive tricks, vandalism, or torching of buildings. No fears of being kidnapped or molested. No trips to
the local hospital to have our candy x-rayed. Just fun and
adventure, that's all.

And I think for most people, then and now, that's the
purpose of Halloween. While we should be very aware of
the dangers and darkness that can accompany Halloween,
I don't think we need to overreact or ruin the innocent fun
that most children, teens, and even adults experience on
this day.

And we shouldn't neglect the many ways that Halloween
can be returned to its Christian heritage. For example, it

provides a great opportunity for creative family activities. We can engage in some charitable activity that benefits others, especially children who don't have the luxury of collecting candy. We can take time to learn about the martyrs and saints whose memory started the Christian observance. And, most of all, after celebrating Halloween, we can be sure to attend Holy Mass on All Saints Day, a holy day of obligation, to honor the saints and pray for the day when we'll finally move from the evil and darkness of the secular world into the goodness and light of God's Kingdom.

CHAPTER 25

Analyzing Rudolph

Throughout your life you've probably been working under the unfortunate misconception that "Rudolph" is nothing more than a cute little Christmas song for children. However, a careful in-depth analysis has revealed that this little ditty is in fact a powerful parable, filled with poignant, if obscure, psychological, sociological, and theological themes.

For example, we find that because Rudolph was different, with a "red, very shiny nose," he was an outcast relegated to the margins of society and rejected by his own peer group. The other reindeer "used to laugh and call him names." One can only wonder what this did for poor Rudolph's psyche and self-esteem. How many nights did he cry himself to sleep, his tears freezing to his pillow in the frigid North Pole air? How many sessions of intense psychotherapy did Rudolph need before he was able to climb out of the depths of his emotional abyss?

The song affirms the value of strong and wise leadership. It was Santa who intervened in the reindeer squabble and saved the day, recognizing that what some saw as a liability could be turned into an asset. It was precisely because Rudolph had a "bright and shiny nose" he was able to cut through the dense fog of Christmas Eve and guarantee the prompt delivery of the much-anticipated and long-awaited Christmas packages. No wonder Santa emerged as the "Alpha Male" of the pack. His ability to effectively use limited resources and build a diverse and cynical herd into an efficient team is to be recognized and applauded.

"Rudolph" is a reminder of how fickle the crowd can be, swaying with the wind, forming its opinions and actions not on personal conviction but on peer pressure. Notice, at the beginning of the song, the negative influence of the gang mentality. The inconsiderate reindeer dismissed Rudolph as a social misfit. Now all of a sudden, in light of his new found success, they "loved him" and enshrined him in the reindeer hall of fame. "You'll go down in history," they shouted shamelessly climbing aboard Rudolph's band-wagon. Rudolph had every right to say, "Sure Dasher and Dancer, Donner and Blitzen, now you're my friends. But where were you when I needed you?"

In that light, the song is a soaring tribute to courage and perseverance. What if Rudolph had become depressed over the unusual condition of his nose? What if he had given up when his friends made fun of him? But he didn't. He stood his ground and waited patiently, confident that his time would come. And did it ever. He and Santa made a formidable team, and in saving Christmas Eve, Rudolph's vindication was complete. Truly a happy ending to what could have been a very sad story.

Well, in offering this analysis I hope I haven't ruined "Rudolph" for you, because it is a nice part of the holiday tradition, especially for children. And all silliness aside, the story of Rudolph does contain some themes that resonate with the true meaning of Christmas.

Like Rudolph, we all have some imperfections or weaknesses that tend to hold us back or even set us apart from others. Perhaps, in the eyes of our peers, we're not very important or successful. But God sees something good in each of us and knows that through the power of grace our liabilities can be turned into something positive. God loves each one of us with an enormous love and it is for that reason He sent His Son to earth – to be with us, to walk with us, to love us, and to save us. Though we might "not go down in history" like Rudolph, even better, we have the hope of eternal life. The birth of Jesus is an affirmation of the significance and dignity each one of us has in the sight of God!

To all of our readers, I offer my sincere best wishes and prayers for a blessed and joyful Christmas season. May the birth of the Christ Child be for you a source of grace, peace and personal affirmation, now and always.

CHAPTER 26

The Grinch and the Angel

Legend has it that each year at this time the Grinch and the Angel meet to debate the meaning and value of Christmas. "Christmas is a serious problem," said the Grinch, "and should be banned from the face of the earth forever." "Christmas is an important occasion and a wonderful opportunity for the human family," responded the Angel. It should be celebrated by everyone with as much joy as possible!"

And so, as the debate began, the Grinch was the first to state his case.

"First of all," said the Grinch, "you know as well as I do that Christmas has lost its religious meaning and has become a shameless commercial and materialistic spectacle. Think how early the marketing begins. Even before Halloween is over, the stores have displayed their Christmas goods. People spend billions of dollars and even go into debt to buy the most expensive of gifts, the latest fads. Have you noticed that some of the newest electronic games for kids cost $300 and $400? Whatever happened to teddy bears and baby dolls? Tell me what this commercial excess has to do with the Birth of Christ.

"The second problem with Christmas," said the Grinch "is that the season becomes so busy, so hectic, no one really enjoys it. The stores are packed with shoppers and the roads are clogged with traffic. The lines are long and tempers are short. Everyone's in a hurry, everyone's anxious.

Christmas is nothing more than an excuse for a month-long party. There's a full schedule of fashionable cocktail parties and dinners, but really, is anyone having fun? People eat too much and drink too much, all the while resolving to lose weight after the holidays."

The Grinch pressed on. "It's all so superficial. Despite the partying and so-called 'good cheer,' Christmas is a really depressing time for lots of people. The expectations are way too high and never met. Think about the people who have to deal with serious illness, the recent death of a loved one, a major family problem or financial crisis. Christmas is anything but merry for them. They just want to survive the holidays and return to some degree of normalcy in their lives."

"And keep in mind that many people don't accept the meaning of Christmas. Not everyone's a Christian; they don't believe that Jesus was the Son of God and Savior of the world. For them the Christmas story is a myth, nothing more than a heart-warming fairy tale. Even the word 'Christmas' is offensive. We don't dare say 'Merry Christmas' any more, but rather, 'Happy Holidays.' Nativity scenes are banned from public squares and buildings, as they should be. Really, how do you Christians get away with taking one of your beliefs, making it a public holiday, and imposing it on others?"

"My final objection," said the Grinch, "is that even some people who pretend to be religious are really hypocrites. Sure they pack the churches on Christmas and, I guess Easter, but where are they the rest of the year? If they really believed the message of Christmas, wouldn't they be consistent in the practice of their faith? Wouldn't they be in church every Sunday?"

"And Christmas sure brings out the Good Samaritans, doesn't it? How many do-gooders visit hospitals and nursing homes at Christmas to sing carols and pass out cookies, but never see the inside of those institutions the rest of the year? And what about those who toss a few coins into the Salvation Army kettle and think they're doing their duty? Really, I wonder if people do these good deeds at Christmas because they're really concerned about others or just to make themselves feel better?"

The Grinch concluded. "That's all I have to say. I'm sorry to sound so negative, but really, Christmas is a disaster. It does more harm than good and we'd all be much better-off without it. Christmas? Bah humbug!"

"You certainly got up on the wrong side of the bed today," said the Angel to the Grinch. "You're even crankier than usual! However, I understand your complaints about Christmas and once again you've made a compelling case. But I'm eager to respond even though I'll never change your mind!"

"It's true," began the Angel, "that the celebration of Christmas has become way too materialistic and I worry about that too. I wish people would avoid the commercial extravagance of Christmas, strive for simplicity, and think more of the spiritual meaning of the day. But on the other hand, remember that the gifts people buy, even if too expensive, are given to family, friends, and neighbors to express love and appreciation. So even if people do spend too much, at least give them a little credit for good intentions."

"I also agree that the Christmas season becomes very busy and people tend to get tired and anxious. It's very important to find some time to rest and relax, to pray about the meaning of the season. But lots of people find a great deal of joy and excitement in all the activity. Their spirits are lifted by the sights and sounds of Christmas, by the lights and the songs, the gift wrap and cards, the cookies and candy – and even the much-maligned fruitcake."

"Of course during the holidays there are parties and dinners – maybe too many, but remember that every time people come together it's an opportunity to renew friendships and strengthen bonds, especially with family and friends who don't meet too often during the year. You should relax a little Grinch, and have some fun during the holidays. It would be good for you!"

The Angel continued.

"I think you're wrong in believing that Christmas exposes the hypocrisy of people. Oh, it's true that there are a few folks who go to church only at Christmastime, and indeed it would be good if they went more often. But perhaps those who attend only at Christmas are a bit like the shepherds and the Magi, traveling to the crib in Bethlehem to see what all the excitement is about. I like to think they're looking for some direction or meaning in their lives. It's always possible, after all, that they'll experience something at Christmas that will touch their hearts and change their lives forever."

"Likewise for charity. Isn't it of some value that at least this one time of the year people are more aware of the less fortunate and try to respond with some good and gentle deeds? Maybe it will open their eyes and inspire them to be more charitable the rest of the year. And besides, my friend, you shouldn't be so critical of others. It wouldn't hurt you to practice a little charity, you know!"

"You are correct, Grinch, not all people are Christians and don't believe that Jesus, born in Bethlehem, was the Son of God. Of course we should respect the beliefs of others, but we shouldn't hesitate for one moment to share our heartfelt convictions with them either. After all, Christmas proclaims good news. The themes of Christmas –hope, joy, and peace – are universal themes and can be appreciated by all people of goodwill. And you'll agree, I'm sure, that our world really needs to hear a little good news now as much as ever."

"Finally," said the Angel, "the message of Christmas is this: that God believes in you, Grinch, even if you don't believe in Him. The birth of Jesus is a reminder that someone loves you even if you are an unlovable old cuss."

And so...having once again debated to a stalemate, the Angel and the Grinch parted company. "Merry Christmas, Grinch," said the Angel. "Happy Holiday, Angel," said the Grinch."

CHAPTER 27

The Christian Family: A Burden or Blessing?

Throughout the celebration of the Christmas mystery, we often pause before the *presepio* to fix our gaze on the Holy Family – Jesus, Mary, and Joseph. We prayerfully reflect on their unique role in salvation history. We admire their steadfast courage. We long to imitate their undaunted love for one another. As a prayer in the liturgy for the Feast of the Holy Family says: "Eternal Father, we want to live as Jesus, Mary, and Joseph, in peace with you and one another."

I don't know, but it seems to me that the example and virtues of the Holy Family become more important each year, especially since we're living in such a pagan culture that does all it can to undermine the fundamental institution of Christian family life.

Consider the following facets of our modern world to illustrate the challenges we face:

- Some segments of our society question the very nature and necessity of marriage as a permanent, life-giving union of one man and one woman.

- Divorce is widely accepted now, even fashionable in some quarters, for Catholics and non-Catholics alike.
- Prenuptial agreements are routinely signed as a type of "insurance policy" for failed marriages.
- Vulnerable, impressionable children grow up in very confusing blended-families.
- Some people consider children to be a burden, a problem to be solved, rather than a gift and blessing of Almighty God.

Relevant to that point, I recall seeing a magazine article with the headline "A Second Kid is Double Trouble for Working Parents." It explained "The arrival of a second child is a pivotal point for many dual career couples, upsetting their careful balance of work and home. Stress multiplies exponentially, fueled by the new complexities in the family and the varied demands of two kids and two jobs."

You see how we tend to blame children for the problems and stress of modern life? How dare a child come into our lives and "upset the delicate balance of work and home." And I wonder how many of us would be around today if our parents had planned for only one or two children?

In this context it's important to affirm some basic Catholic teachings about marriage and the family. We believe that marriage, as instituted by God and raised to a sacrament by Jesus Christ, is a permanent, exclusive, life-giving union of one man and one woman. We believe that sexual activity is morally acceptable only within the context of matrimony. We believe that sexual activity within marriage is ordered to the love-giving unity of the spouses and the life-giving procreation of children. We believe that artificial means of contraception are contrary to God's design for human sexuality and objectively wrong. We believe that human life is sacred, from the moment of conception to the moment of natural death. We believe that children are a wonderful gift of God, not an intrusion to be managed or a problem to be solved!

When Pope Paul VI visited Nazareth in 1964 he spoke eloquently about the example of the Holy Family: "In the Holy Family of Nazareth, we learn about family life. Nazareth serves as a model of what family life should be. May it show us the family's holy and enduring character and illustrate its basic function in society – to be a community of love and sharing, beautiful for the problems it poses and the rewards it brings. In sum, it is the perfect setting for rearing children, and for this there is no substitute."

In saying that the family is a "community of love and sharing" we affirm that all the members of the family, parents and children, are joined in a steadfast commitment to love and thus share the joys and sorrows, the victories and defeats, the successes and failures of the other members.

And, the Pope reminds us, the family is "a perfect setting for rearing children" a statement of the obvious that is even more relevant now than it was forty years ago!

In this holy season we shouldn't minimize the fact that God, in His wisdom, chose to send His Son into a human family so that in His human nature Jesus would experience all the blessings and challenges the human community could give. As we navigate the turbulent waters of our secular culture we need to consider the example of the Holy Family. In this New Year, renew your commitment to your family and strive to make it another "holy family." And, let's be sure to pray for all the good people whose experience of family life has been less than perfect, that they may nonetheless discover the beauty of God's grace and the wisdom of His provident plan.

CHAPTER 28

A Christmas Gift for the Dalai Lama

What to buy for a man who has little and wants even less? That's the question I've pondered ever since I met the Dalai Lama last month at Salve Regina University in Newport, Rhode Island.

First I should say, very sincerely, that it was a privilege to meet the Dalai Lama. He is a renowned and impressive figure, the head of state and the spiritual leader of the Tibetan people. He travels the world to meet with popes and presidents. When he speaks of peace and justice, people listen. For his commitment to a non-violent liberation of Tibet from China he was awarded the Nobel Peace Prize in 1989.

His appearance at Salve Regina University was a result of his longtime friendship with former Rhode Island Senator Claiborne Pell after whom "The Claiborne Pell Center" at the University is named. It was an historic moment for Salve Regina, a stunning accomplishment for its leader, Sister M. Therese Antone, R.S.M., and a wonderful opportunity for the students and members of the surrounding community. Upon meeting the Dalai Lama I knew, without a doubt, that I had encountered a good and holy man.

The theme of the Dalai Lama's talk was "A human approach to world peace," and his message was simple but profound. In clear, unassuming and sometimes metaphorical language, he spoke of the importance of fostering positive emotions, instead of negative emotions. He taught that the key to world peace is personal, interior peace. Inner peace spreads to families, and then to the community, and eventually to the whole world. Compassion, understanding, and tolerance are the building blocks of a humane society. Patience is essential, he reminded the young and idealistic college students, lest they become discouraged by the lack of peace and justice in the world around them.

The Dalai Lama's message was well received by the rapt audience and it warmed the cold and breezy tent in which we huddled.

I need to confess, however, that I came away from the presentation with a feeling of emptiness, almost sadness. The Dalai Lama's message was wonderful, but incomplete. "There was no core to his teaching," another listener observed. Upon reflection I realized that what was missing was any reference to a personal God, any reference to the Lord Jesus Christ.

The Dalai Lama, of course, was just being true to his own religious principles, a tradition that doesn't emphasize salvation by a personal God. For Buddhists, the path of "enlightenment" results in "nirvana," a state of detachment from the world which is the source of evil. In Buddhism there is no earthly discourse between God and His people, no incarnation of God's Eternal Word, no personal redemption in the death and resurrection of a Savior, and no union with a loving God in heaven. It is for this reason that Pope John Paul in his memoirs spoke of Buddhism as an "atheistic system" – not to disparage a noble religious tradition, but simply to identify the source and goal of its mystical instinct.

In listening to the Dalai Lama I thought of St. Paul's address to the Athenians as recorded in *The Acts of the Apostles*: "I see that in every respect you are very religious. For as I walked around looking carefully at your shrines, I even discovered an altar inscribed, 'To an Unknown God.' What therefore you unknowingly worship, I proclaim to you. The God who made the world and all that is in it, the Lord of heaven and earth…it is he who gives to everyone life and breath and everything." (Cf. Acts 17: 22-31)

Christians believe that Jesus Christ is the revelation of the "Unknown God," or as St. Paul wrote, the "image of the invisible God." (Col 1:15) The Gospel of St. John explains the universal nature of salvation in Jesus Christ: "For God so loved the world that he gave his only Son, so that everyone who believes in him might not perish but might have eternal life. For God did not send his Son into the world to condemn the world, but that the world might be saved through him." (Jn 3:16-17)

For that reason the Church teaches that "It must be firmly believed as a truth of Catholic faith that the universal will of the One and Triune God is offered and accomplished once for all in the mystery of the incarnation, death and resurrection of the Son of God." And again, "One can and must say that Jesus Christ has a significance and a value for the human race and its history, which are unique and singular, proper to Him alone, exclusive, universal, and absolute." (*Dominus Jesus, #14-15*)

In short, no one can replace Jesus Christ and without Him every religious experience is imperfect. He is the Savior of all people, those who believe in Him and those who don't.

So, I think I've found the perfect Christmas gift for the Dalai Lama. With respect and affection, I would like to give him Jesus, because Jesus is the fulfillment of the love and compassion, the peace and justice of which the Dalai Lama spoke so well.

Our Final Days

During the Season of Advent, soon upon us, our thoughts and prayers focus on the Second Coming of Christ when, at the end of time, He will return in glory. Advent, then, is an opportunity to recall what the Church teaches us about the end of times – heaven, hell, purgatory, limbo, the Second Coming of Christ, and the Final Judgment.

Heaven is the easiest to talk about since it's the destination we desire and presume to attain. Of course that presumption can be deadly to our spiritual welfare, especially if we take our salvation for granted or get lazy in the practice of our faith.

The *Catechism of the Catholic Church* explains: "Those who die in God's grace and friendship are perfectly purified and live forever with Christ. (#1023) "This perfect life with the Most Holy Trinity – this communion of life and love with the Trinity, with the Virgin Mary, the angels and all the blessed – is called 'heaven'..." (#1024)

There are, of course, a few things we don't know about heaven: Will we get bored in heaven? Will we see our loved ones? Are there pets in heaven? These questions about heaven, and about the other final destinations, will undoubtedly remain a mystery until the end.

Purgatory is one of the most particular of Catholic beliefs. "All who die in God's grace and friendship, but still imperfectly purified, are indeed assured of their eternal salvation; but after death they undergo purification, so as to achieve the holiness necessary to enter the joy of heaven." (#1030) "The Church gives the name *Purgatory* to this final purification of the elect which is entirely different from the punishment of the damned." (#1031)

When you think about it, it is only this belief in purgatory that explains our practice of praying for the dead. After all, the souls in heaven don't need our prayers; the souls in hell can't benefit from our prayers. "Thus he made atonement for the dead that they might be freed from this sin." (2 Macc 12:46)

Hell is a topic and most assuredly a destination we'd rather avoid. Some deny that hell even exists, arguing that a merciful God could never condemn His creatures to an eternity of unspeakable suffering. But Jesus often spoke about hell, and the Church's teaching is very clear.

"To die in mortal sin without repenting and accepting God's merciful love means remaining separated from Him forever by our own free choice. This state of definitive self-exclusion from communion with God and the blessed is called 'hell'." (#1033) More to the point, "Immediately after death the souls of those who die in a state of moral sin descend into hell where they suffer the punishments of hell, 'eternal fire'." (#1035)

Limbo has returned to the news recently but traditionally has been regarded as the outskirts (in Latin, *limbus*) of heaven where, according to one theological opinion, the souls of children who die without Baptism are gathered.

The idea of limbo has never been defined as part of the Catholic Faith and as the *Catechism* states and recent theological statements have affirmed, "As regards children who have died without Baptism, the Church can only entrust them to the mercy of God." (#1261)

Now, that's a summary of the stops along our final journey. But what do Catholics believe about the judgment we receive as we pass from this life to eternity? Well, in short, we believe in both a Particular Judgment and a Final Judgment.

The **Particular Judgment** occurs at the moment of death. "The New Testament speaks of judgment primarily in its aspect of the final encounter with Christ in his second coming, but also repeatedly affirms that each will be rewarded immediately after death in accordance with his works and faith." (#1021) "Each man receives his eternal retribution in his immortal soul at the very moment of his death, in a particular judgment that refers his life of Christ: either entrance into the blessedness of heaven – through a purification or immediately – or immediate and everlasting damnation." (#1022)

The **Last Judgment** will take place when Christ returns in glory. "In the presence of Christ, who is Truth itself, the truth of each man's relationship with God will be laid bare. The Last Judgment will reveal even to its further consequences the good each person has done or failed to do during his earthly life." (#1039) At the Last Judgment "we shall know the ultimate meaning of the whole work of creation and the entire economy of salvation and understand the marvelous ways by which his Providence led everything towards its final end." (#1040)

Catholic belief about the **Second Coming of Christ** can be summarized as follows: That Christ will return to the earth as the glorious Son of Man to judge all mankind; that the second coming of Christ will be unmistakable because it will be accompanied by unprecedented signs in the heavens and on earth; that no one — "neither the angels in heaven, nor the Son," (Mk 13:32) knows when the second coming of Christ will occur; and, finally, that Christians should always be prepared for Christ's coming and live their lives in such a way that they can look forward to His return with joyful hope, rather than fear.

Patience and prayer, hope and joy – these are virtues that should mark the life of every Christian as we await the Second Coming of Christ as well as our observance of Advent.

Faith Through the Life of the Church

CHAPTER 30

Theology in 30
Seconds or Less

The concluding moments of a recent television interview went something like this . . .

"*Well, Bishop Tobin, we have just about 30 seconds left today, time for one last question . . . We've been hearing that the Vatican is studying the possibility of allowing the use of condoms in places where AIDS is rampant. This would be a major change in Catholic teaching, wouldn't it? What would it mean for Catholics? What's your reaction to this possibility?*"

"*Um . . .*" I said. "*Of course it's a very complex question and we'll just have to wait and see what the Vatican says.*"

"*Thank you Bishop Tobin. Well that wraps up the show for today, folks. Be sure to join us again next week . . .*"

In describing this scene, I should mention, first of all, that I sincerely enjoyed doing the interview. The two reporters were thoroughly professional and well-prepared, very kind and gracious. I'd do the show again in a heartbeat, if asked to do so.

Nevertheless, I departed the TV studio a little confused, feeling that I hadn't explained the teachings of the Church very well, especially in responding to the last, really loaded question. But how could I, in 30 seconds or less?

How could I begin to explain the complexities of Catholic moral theology related to the thorny issue of condoms and AIDS: The foundations of Christian morality in Scripture, Tradition and Natural Law; The principle of double-effect; Intention and proportionality; Cooperation in evil, material and formal; The purposes of marriage and the evil of contraception?

I suspect that someday I'll have to explain a newspaper headline that says something like: "Vatican approves condom use" – four simple words that don't begin to tell the whole truth.

Catholic theology doesn't fare well when it's reduced to 30 second interviews or four-word newspaper headlines. It has far too much history; it's much too complicated, rich, and nuanced for that. But in our media-driven culture, when many people don't get beyond the headlines or sound bites, that's the reality of the situation.

Another example. The headline shouts: "Vatican bars gays from seminaries."

Again, a complicated issue. The headline doesn't explain that the recent Vatican document is one in a long series of statements on priestly formation dating back 40 years; that, in effect, it simply ratified a current practice; that indeed some homosexual men can be admitted to the seminary and be ordained priests under certain conditions; that all Christians are called to chastity; that there are positive reasons for priestly celibacy.

Think of other contemporary headlines, all within the realm of possibility, that beg for more nuance and understanding.

"Catholic politicians barred from Communion."

"Church covers up sexual abuse."

"Dissident theologian excommunicated."

"Church condemns stem cell research."

"Vatican says no to women priests."

"Bishop embraces illegal immigrants."

"Church abandons concept of limbo."

You get the point, I'm sure. While there may be some degree of truth in each of these headlines, the stories are far more complicated than the headlines suggest.

I know there's no easy answer to this dilemma. Newspapers will continue to introduce complicated stories with facile headlines, and television interviews will continue to utilize 30 second sound bites to approach the most difficult of issues. I guess it's unavoidable. For that reason, though, you need to approach the secular media with extreme caution, especially when it delves into religious and spiritual topics well beyond its normal competence.

And by the way, I'm not one who believes that the secular media and the Church are natural enemies. While it's true that sometimes media people actively promote their own secular agenda, at other times they simply don't grasp the meaning of religious issues and events. More often than not people from the various media seek to be fair and does a pretty good job. And if truth be told, sometimes the Church doesn't understand and respect the professional responsibilities of the media either.

Nonetheless, it points to the fact that Catholics, and other interested parties, need to go beyond the headlines, and even the stories themselves, to achieve a better understanding of the faith, particularly as it applies to contemporary issues. It's important for members of the Church to be well-informed: to attend continuing education classes and lectures; to study *The Catechism of the Catholic Church* and other Church documents; to read Catholic newspapers and periodicals; and to discuss the complicated issues of the day with people who know what they're talking about.

Understanding the entire truth of a complex situation is essential for the practice of our faith and personal spiritual growth. It's also important so that we can clearly explain to others the depth and richness of our Catholic Faith.

"Catholic Church teaches truth and serves humanity." Now, that's a headline I'd like to see.

CHAPTER 31

Godparents: Helpers on the Road of Faith

Without a doubt Baptism is an important and joyful occasion – for the person being baptized, members of the family, and the entire Church community. In preparing for Baptism, however, one of the first questions parents encounter is the selection of godparents. It's about the choice and role of godparents that I write today. But first, a few words about the meaning of Baptism.

Baptism, of course, is the primary sacrament of the Christian Faith, the foundation upon which the entire Christian life is built. When we're baptized, the original sin with which we are born as children of Adam and Eve is taken away, we are filled with sanctifying grace, and we become members of the Church, the Body of Christ.

But Baptism is only a beginning! For Baptism to achieve its full potential, it has to be followed by a lifetime of grace and faith. In presenting their child for Baptism, parents promise to practice the Catholic Faith and to do everything possible to share their faith with their children. How sad and inconsistent it is when parents request Baptism for their children and then walk away from the Church with little or no intention of returning anytime soon.

Supporting parents in the practice of the faith is the particular responsibility of the godparents of the child being baptized. Sometimes, however, it seems that the role of godparents is not properly understood, even by practicing Catholics. (For the sake of simplicity here I use the term "godparent" and "sponsor" interchangeably.)

First, a word about what godparents should *not* be. The role of godparent is not an honor given to a favorite aunt, uncle, or lifetime friend. ("I've known John forever, he's a really great guy and I want him to be the godfather of my child.") Nor is it a reward in exchange for another favor. ("I was the maid-of-honor at her wedding and I want to thank her by asking her to be my baby's godmother.") Nor does it entail the bestowal of a legal right or duty to raise the child to adulthood should "something happen" to the parents.

Being a godparent for Baptism is a serious spiritual responsibility and a commitment of faith. (All that we say here about Baptism sponsors also applies to Confirmation sponsors by the way.)

Because it is such an important role, the *Code of Canon Law* describes some of the requirements for being a Baptism sponsor.

First it reminds us that, "Only one male or one female sponsor, or one of each sex is to be employed." (#873) It is not permissible to have two godfathers or two godmothers.

The next Canon (#874) lists the specific requirements for being a sponsor, which can be summarized as follows:

- Normally be at least 16 years old;
- Have already received the three sacraments of initiation: Baptism, Confirmation and Eucharist;
- Be a Catholic in good standing, someone who leads a life in harmony with the Catholic Faith;
- Not be the parents of the person being baptized.

The *Catechism of the Catholic Church* offers a broader, more pastoral description of the role of godparents: "For the grace of Baptism to unfold, the parents' help is important. So too is the role of the godfather and godmother, who must be firm believers, able, and ready to help the newly baptized – child or adult – on the road of Christian life." (#1255)

This description is reflected in the Baptism ceremony when the celebrant turns to the godparents and asks, "Are you ready to help the parents of this child in their duty as Christian parents?" And they respond, "We are." And later in the Rite the godparents join the parents in "renouncing Satan, his works and all his empty promises" and professing their faith on behalf of the one being baptized.

All of this emphasizes that the role of the godparent goes well beyond the ceremony itself; it's meant to last a lifetime. What does the *Catechism* mean, exactly, when it says that godparents must be "firm believers, able and ready to help the newly baptized on the road of Christian life?"

Well, the Christian life is just that – a road, a journey, a pilgrimage, and with so many challenges, temptations, and distractions these days it can be a very difficult road to travel. Every Christian needs the example and support of the community, represented especially by their godparents, if they are to travel the Christian highway safely and successfully.

In practical terms, then, that means that godparents must be faithful members of the Church, regularly attending Mass and receiving the sacraments, especially the Holy Eucharist and Reconciliation.

Godparents should give a good example of a moral life, keeping the Commandments of the Lord and the precepts of the Church. Their lives should be shining examples of integrity, charity, justice, and compassion.

Godparents should try to be present to the person they've sponsored, praying for them and with them, affirming them in the practice of the Christian Faith and even challenging them if they're ever tempted to leave the "road of the Christian life."

That's a pretty serious job description, isn't it? Nonetheless, that's exactly what's involved in being a sacramental sponsor in the Church.

So, if at some point you need to choose godparents for your child, choose carefully, with these points in mind. And if you're asked to be a godparent, congratulations – it's a real honor and privilege. But before you accept the invitation, be sure you're willing and able to live up to the expectations your position demands.

CHAPTER 32

Catholic Preaching: Powerful or Pitiful?

You've probably heard the story of the little boy who, with his family, was greeting the parish priest after Sunday Mass. "Father," said the lad, "when I grow up I'm going to give you all the money I have!" "Well that's very nice," said the priest, "but why would you do a thing like that?" The boy responded, "Because my dad just said that you're the poorest preacher we've ever had!"

I thought of that story recently when I saw a *Catholic News Service* article entitled, "Homilies: What makes for a good one?" The article reports the results of a survey in the Diocese of Wilmington, Delaware, that underlines the importance of homilies to the faith formation of Catholics. "Homilies are far and away the single most important source for 97 percent of our adults," said the Director of Religious Education. Another person responded that a good homily is "something that resonates with my faith, something that makes me go a little deeper and connects to the faith with honesty."

So that leads to the question of the day: What makes for a good homily?

Recognizing that some critics will respond, "Physician, heal thyself," let me propose four qualities of good homilies.

First, a good homily must be firmly rooted in the Word of God and completely consistent with the teachings of the Church.

The recent Vatican Instruction, *Redemptionis Sacramentum* explains that homilies should "be based upon the mysteries of salvation, expounding the mysteries of the faith and norms for Christian life from the biblical readings and liturgical texts."

Why is this principle an essential ingredient of a good homily? Well, because it ensures that the preaching of the Word will be an authentic act of the Church and not the personal whimsy of the individual preacher. No one goes to church to hear a barrage of personal opinions. The faithful who attend Mass need and deserve to hear the Word of God in all of its power and beauty, just as it's been handed down through the generations.

Second, a good homily must be relevant to the people who hear it.

While it has to be consistent with sound theological principles, a homily is not a theology lecture. A good homily attempts to make a clear connection – between God's Word and the circumstances of everyday life.

The lack of relevance in Sunday homilies is a complaint I often receive from the pews. Catholics want their preachers to address issues they hear about every day, issues that touch their lives – war and peace, abortion, stem cell research, human sexuality, marriage and family, care of the poor, the challenges of the contemporary Church. The Word of God has something to say about all of these things and the faithful want to know what it is.

Third, a good homily is passionate.

One of the best pieces of advice I received about preaching, from a student just ahead of me in the seminary, is as important as it is obvious: Never say anything you don't really mean. But the corollary is also true – if you believe something, say it like you mean it!

So much of Catholic preaching today is, quite simply, bland and boring. Some of the homilies I hear on nationally televised Masses are so bad that the Weather Channel is inspiring by comparison. As Catholics we have a wonderful message to share, we possess truths that can change the world and save souls. But if we really believe the truth of our message why are we so boring? Where's the fire, where's the conviction, where's the passion of our preaching?

Finally, a good homily is memorable.

By this I mean that a homily will be illustrated in a way that helps listeners recall the message. Jesus used parables and illustrations from everyday life to explain the mysteries of the Kingdom of God. In today's culture of round-the-clock entertainment and short attention spans, it's important for preachers to use similar techniques – parables, real life incidents, references to current events and humor – to illustrate the message they're trying to convey. In that way listeners will have something tangible to store in their memories and recall during the week. (Admittedly there's a danger in overdoing it. Who hasn't been turned off a preacher who thinks he's a stand-up comedian and, sadly, loses the message in the medium?)

So . . . next time you're with a group of Catholics and the conversation starts to lag, just ask the question, "How's the preaching in your parish, powerful or pitiful?" Without a doubt, you'll get an earful!

CHAPTER 33

The Gospel at 30,000 Feet

"I've never had the chance to talk to a priest before," said the young lady sitting next to me, "but if I don't ask you some questions right now I'll probably explode and have to see my therapist tonight."

That was the intriguing beginning of a rather intense dialogue I had with a fellow passenger while flying to the Bishops' meeting in Chicago last summer.

I should explain, first of all, that I don't like to talk to people while I'm traveling, even when I'm wearing a Roman collar. I prefer to read, rest and relax, and not engage in heavy, sometimes awkward discussions. In fact, sometimes when I travel, especially for vacation, I dress casually, in secular clothes, just to stay below the radar screen.

That didn't happen on my flight to Chicago and my collar attracted my interviewer like a moth to a flame.

Before I agreed to answer her questions, I decided to learn a little about the young lady who had stared at me throughout the flight, even while I was pretending to sleep. I discovered that she was 16 years old, a member of a devout Orthodox Jewish family. Her upbringing was sheltered, she explained, and thus it was that she had never met a Catholic priest before. She attended an Orthodox Jewish School in Chicago. "Do you enjoy school?" I asked. "I hate it," she said, revealing that she was a lot more like other teenagers than she knew.

"Okay," I said, holding my breath. "What are your questions?"

"Well," she began, "you guys believe that if you're not a Christian you can't get to heaven, right?" (I learned pretty quickly that "you guys" could refer to Christians, Catholics, priests or bishops, depending on the question.)

I tried to explain, briefly, that while we believe that Jesus Christ is the Savior of all people, and that there is something very special about being Catholic, that if people are true to their own consciences, they can indeed be saved even if they're not Christian – whether they be Jewish, Muslim, Buddhist, Hindu or anything else.

"Cool," she said.

Other questions quickly followed.

"Why are you going to Chicago? You're a bishop? Oh my gosh, my mom will never believe it. Do you wear that thing (meaning my Roman collar) all the time? Do you always carry a Bible with you? What do you think of the new Pope? My friends and I really liked Pope John Paul. We thought he was cute and he had Jewish friends. But we're not sure about the new guy. Don't you think you should get married? After all, if everybody was like you there wouldn't be any children. If priests are so holy, why did they abuse so many kids?

Isn't Lent when you guys (there it is again) get ready for Christmas, or is it Easter? And don't you give up something for Lent? Why do you do that? What do you give up?" At which point another young lady sitting directly behind us piped up, without invitation, "I always give up candy, but it's really hard, because I like chocolate."

I realized now that other passengers were listening intently to our conversation, no doubt enjoying the sound of me squirming. "Will she get a higher place in heaven because she gave up candy?" asked my new friend without missing a beat. "By the way, you didn't tell me . . . what do you give up for Lent?"

About this time, a truly blessed voice from heaven came to the rescue: "In preparation for our landing in Chicago . . ." "Thank you, Lord," I prayed, having never been so happy before to hear the standard message. My personal inquisition had come to an end and I breathed a sigh of relief as I departed the plane.

Upon later reflection, I concluded that, despite the awkward circumstances of our personal interfaith dialogue, I had probably accomplished some good. I hoped that my young traveling companion would remember her first encounter with a Catholic priest as a positive experience. I had provided accurate information about our faith, and, perhaps, dispelled some misperceptions she had harbored for a long time.

Jesus said, "Go forth and teach" and indeed we have opportunities to teach, to share our faith with family and friends, co-workers and neighbors, everyday, sometimes with words, but always with good deeds and example.

My conversation with a young Jewish friend reminded me that it is possible to spread the Gospel anytime and anyplace, even at 30,000 feet.

CHAPTER 34

What's the Best Age for Confirmation?

I've been thinking a lot about Confirmation recently, for a couple of different reasons.

First, because as a diocese we're nearing the end of another "Confirmation Season." Although the schedule can be daunting sometimes, I certainly enjoy visiting our parishes for Confirmation. Once again I extend my congratulations to the young people who have been confirmed as well as their sponsors and families. I applaud all those who have prepared the Confirmation candidates. And I want to express a very sincere word of gratitude to our senior bishops who are so generous with their time in assisting with Confirmation ceremonies. Their presence and ministry is a real gift to our local Church.

Second, I've been thinking about Confirmation because of something our Holy Father Pope Benedict XVI wrote about the sacrament in his recent letter on the Eucharist, *Sacramentum Caritatis*. There, in describing the relationship of the Eucharist to the other sacraments, the Pope wrote: "It must never be forgotten that our reception of Baptism and Confirmation is ordered to the Eucharist.

In this regard, attention needs to be paid to the order of the sacraments of initiation . . . In close collaboration with the competent offices of the Roman Curia, Bishops' Conferences should examine the effectiveness of current approaches to Christian initiation." (#17-18)

When I read those words all sorts of bells and whistles went off in my head. The net effect of what the Holy Father is saying is that once again we need to examine whether Confirmation should go before or after First Communion, and, therefore, what the most appropriate age for Confirmation is. And I said to myself, "Here we go again!"

I remember an experienced bishop telling me that there are three things that the Bishops of the United States can never agree on: The number of national collections; the holy days of obligation, and the age of Confirmation. Indeed as the Holy Father points out, when it comes to Confirmation, "Different traditions exist within the Church . . . Yet these variations are not properly of the dogmatic order, but are pastoral in character." Therefore, he suggests, it's an issue that can and should be studied.

When it comes to the age for the reception of Confirmation, there are three current practices in the Western Church. Each has its advantages and disadvantages.

The first is to place Confirmation before First Holy Communion. This means that youngsters are confirmed at or about the age of seven. A few dioceses of the country have already adopted this practice. The advantage of this arrangement is that it "restores the original order of the sacraments" and leads to the Eucharist as the culmination of initiation in the Church. The disadvantage of this practice is that it requires us to prepare children to receive three sacraments, including Reconciliation, at a very early age and in a relatively short period of time.

(Now, far be it from me to disagree with the Pope or other experts in the field, but for a long time I've argued that the real original order of initiation was in fact Eucharist before Confirmation because the Apostles received the Eucharist at the Last Supper before they received the Holy Spirit at Pentecost. If that's the process of "initiation" Jesus used with His Apostles, it's good enough for me.)

The second option for the reception of Confirmation is in the junior high years, about the 7th or 8th grade. The advantage here is that there's an opportunity to catechize the young people about the meaning of the sacrament and that they are old enough to understand what they're doing. Another argument, and I think a compelling one, is that bestowing the gifts of the Holy Spirit upon the youngsters as they enter the teenage years is extremely important since they can be the most dangerous and challenging years of their life. The disadvantage of confirming this age group is that the "original order" of the sacraments is lost and that the youngsters aren't really mature enough to make a serious commitment to their faith.

The third option for the reception of Confirmation is in the high school years, typically between the 10th and 12th grade. The advantage of this age is that the young people are more mature and are able to make a better, a well-informed, commitment to Christ and the Church. Another advantage, (though one that is sometimes questioned) is that it provides parishes with a built-in youth ministry program. The disadvantage of this approach is that by the high school years we've already lost some of the students – they've become independent and busy; they're driving, dating, and working and have grown less interested in the life of the Church. As a result many young people will never be confirmed, a serious problem for the practice of their faith.

I have to confess that personally I favor the second option, the reception of Confirmation in the junior high years, for the positive reasons mentioned above. As a bishop celebrating Confirmation for over 14 years now, I find 8th graders to be a wonderful group to work with – they're receptive, articulate, and growing rapidly. They urgently need the gifts of the Holy Spirit and they present very fertile soil for the reception of God's grace.

CHAPTER 35

What Will the Church Look Like in the Year 2032?

E ven in the midst of my regular schedule there are some special moments in which I am reminded why I was called to the priesthood. Once such moment occurred in 2007 when I had the great joy of welcoming four new priests into the ranks of the Diocese of Providence: Fr. Marcin Mioduszewski, Fr. Richard Narciso, Fr. Albert Ranallo, and Fr. Victor Silva. We are truly blessed to have the service of these talented and dedicated men and we hope and pray that they will have a long, faithful, and joyful ministry in our diocese. I expect that they will.

However, we really don't know what the future will hold for our new priests, do we? We know that they will experience some good times and bad times, moments of joy and sorrow, success and failure, sickness and health, life and death. These experiences are part of everyone's journey on earth. But beyond those generalities, we haven't a clue about what awaits our new priests.

Predicting the future can be a precarious exercise to be sure. I remember someone commenting on the Second Vatican Council and noting the great number of bishops from all over the world who gathered for that historic meeting. The commentator guessed that at the Third Vatican Council the bishops would again assemble, this time accompanied by their wives. And at the Fourth Vatican Council, he predicted, the bishops would gather, now with their husbands. Yikes! Now there's a discussion starter.

But, despite the perils of prognosticating, let's ponder this question: What will the Church in the Diocese of Providence look like in the year 2032 when our new priests will be celebrating their 25th Anniversaries? I don't know, but I can hope . . .

I hope that in 2032 the diocese will have plenty of priests to care for God's People, that our present emphasis on vocations will bear great fruit, and that many young men will come forward to serve the Lord and His Church.

I hope that in 2032 the Permanent Diaconate will continue to be an important resource for our diocese with many men, married and single, assisting their pastors and exercising the works of the apostolate in catechesis, youth ministry, hospitals, nursing homes, and prisons.

I hope that in 2032, the Consecrated life will have experienced a true renewal, a renewal of membership, identity, and mission, and that all of our religious communities will be flourishing, bearing effective witness to the presence of God in the world.

I hope that in 2032 we will have a greater appreciation for the holiness of marriage and family life; that fewer couples will cohabitate before marriage; that the divorce rate will have dropped; and that parents as well as society will recognize children as a blessing, not a burden.

I hope that in 2032 the laity will more fully exercise their particular vocation in the world, that they will be well-prepared and inspired to carry the Gospel of Christ into their personal and professional lives, transforming the secular society into the Kingdom of God.

I hope that in 2032 many more Catholics will be participating regularly in the sacramental life of the Church including attendance at Sunday Mass – every week – and a return to frequent confessions.

I hope that in 2032 our parishes, even if fewer in number or in different locations, will be vibrant communities of worship, education, and service; that our Catholic schools, religious education programs, and youth ministry will be as effective as possible so that we can educate our youngsters and lead them to full participation in the life of the Church.

I hope that in 2032 the Church will live in a world that reveres the sanctity of human life, that abortions will have been virtually eliminated from the face of the earth, and that the Catholic Church will be recognized for its leadership in promoting the Gospel of Life.

I hope that in 2032 the Church will have welcomed and successfully incorporated the many new immigrants who have come to our nation, and that we will be strengthened, not threatened, by the rich diversity of our community.

I hope that in 2032 the Church will have found even more effective ways of serving the poor, the weak, the disenfranchised members of our community, and that concern for the poor will be a hallmark of Catholics everywhere.

Well, Fr. Marcin, Fr. Richard, Fr. Albert and Fr. Victor – that's my hope and prayer for the Church you'll be serving in 25 years. Who knows, it may or may not come to pass. You can save this column and check it out when the time comes. In any event, let me be the first to wish you a happy and blessed Twenty-Fifth Anniversary. If I'm no longer among the living, I'll be celebrating with you from my place in heaven. (I hope!) And if I'm still here, at the ripe old age of 84, please invite me to your celebration. Or at least stop by the nursing home to say hello and give me your blessing.

CHAPTER 36

Why Do We Pray?

Recently U.S. News & World Report ran a cover article on "The Power of Prayer." The introduction said: "Some do it on their knees, and others require beads. Some need a pew in church, while for others the location makes no difference whatsoever. Whatever form it takes, prayer is an essential part of most of the world's religions and has been through the ages."

The report then summarized the results of an Internet survey about prayer in which more than 5,600 people participated.

For starters, 64 percent reported that they pray more than once a day. More than 79 percent say that they pray most often at home, while just 5 percent pray most often in a house of worship. Some 56 percent pray frequently for family members, but only 3.3 percent pray for strangers.

The article described some of the *reasons* for prayer, ranging from the purely spiritual to the very practical. Some pray for Divine inspiration and a closer relationship with God. Others pray to praise God and thank Him for blessings received. One woman prayed for her pet chicken after a dog mauled it -the chicken lived; and another for a car that constantly overheated -the car never overheated again. (These prayers aren't necessarily frivolous. If you've ever had a pet, you understand. And if you depend on your car for your livelihood or to transport children to school, it's a reasonable thing to pray for!)

But it's a good question to explore, even from a Christian perspective: What is the purpose of prayer?

By far, the most frequent motive for prayer is to ask for God's help, for needs large and small. We pray for peace and justice in the world; for victims of natural disasters; for the Church and its leaders; for members of our families; for the faithful departed; for good grades (it's been said that as long as there are tests in schools, there will be prayer in the classrooms); for an engagement ring; to pass a driver's test; for a lucky lottery ticket; and for our favorite football team.

We ask God for favors so often that it's embarrassing. And as we approach the Lord it is helpful to sort out those things that are important from those that aren't. "Ask and it will be given to you; seek and you will find; knock and the door will be opened to you." (Mt 7:7)

Secondly, our prayer is a source and sign of our faith, and a key to holiness. It all begins with the recognition of God's primacy in our lives. Note that in the Lord's Prayer, the emphasis is on God, not us: "Our Father, who art in heaven; hallowed by thy name. Thy kingdom come. Thy will be done." In other words, to maintain our reverence for God and the things of God, to pray for the coming of the kingdom in the world, and to seek to do God's will-aren't these the building blocks of a solid spiritual life?

Regular personal prayer is also an essential ingredient of holiness. St. John Chrysostom said: "Practice prayer from the beginning. Paint your house with the colors of modesty and humility. Make it radiant with the light of justice. Decorate it with the finest gold leaf of good deeds. Adorn it with the walls and stones of faith and generosity. Crown it with the pinnacle of prayer. In this way you will make it a perfect dwelling place for the Lord."

And finally, prayer is an act of solidarity with our brothers and sisters in need. Some fear, perhaps, that intense prayer causes us to withdraw from others, makes us less socially conscious. Not true. Intense prayer never hardens the heart but makes it more aware of and respon-sive to the plight of others. (Some of the most alert and connected people in the world are cloistered, contemplative monks and nuns.) A full Christian life includes both prayer and social action. Without prayer, our apostolic work lacks a solid foundation. But without social action, our prayer is sterile and fruitless.

Blessed Mother Teresa understood very well the value and the intimate relationship of both aspects of the Christian life. She said: "To love with a pure heart, to love everybody, especially to love the poor, is a 24-hour prayer." And again: "Prayer begets faith, faith begets love, and love begets service on behalf of the poor."

So. ..why do people pray? I guess there are just about as many reasons as there are people. The important thing about prayer, though, is not to analyze, scrutinize, and categorize it. The important thing is to just do it.

CHAPTER 37

Now . . . About Your Pastor

*"*A*re you willing to sacrifice an entire parish for the sake of one incompetent, uncaring priest?"*

That's the question presented to me in a letter I received from a parishioner very unhappy with her pastor. I'll attempt to answer the question, but first, a little background.

One of the most important and challenging tasks of a bishop is the assignment of priests. Like most bishops I don't make clergy assignments arbitrarily, but only after careful consideration and consultation with others, including the Priest Personnel Board.

For better or worse, the assignment of priests these days involves the fine art of negotiation. In assigning priests we're obliged to consider, first of all, the pastoral needs of the diocese. A man is ordained with the full understanding, in obedience, that he will be sent by the bishop to serve the needs of the Church wherever they might be.

We also try to evaluate the personal needs and limitations of each priest. A number of questions are considered: Are the unique gifts and talents of this priest suited for this particular parish? Will he get along with the others with whom he will live and work? Will his health allow him to fulfill the duties of his assignment? Is he the primary caregiver of his parents or other family members and will that affect his availability? Sometimes there are other confidential matters not subject to public scrutiny.

More often than not, the faithful of the diocese are very grateful for and supportive of their priests. People are understandably unhappy when a favorite priest is moved. Nonetheless, the transfer of priests is a normal and, I believe, healthy practice for the Church as well as the priests.

Sometimes I receive letters from people who are *not* happy with their priest and they request, even *demand*, that he be transferred. Once in awhile these requests take the form of letter-writing campaigns that quickly become negative and divisive of the parish.

In some cases, I receive letters from both sides – for and against a particular priest. What's a bishop to do?

As you reflect on the assignment of priests, then, I hope you'll consider two points.

The first, and perhaps most obvious, is that priests aren't perfect. We're all aware of a few priests who have fallen short of the mark, who have not lived up to the promises of their ordination day. And not all priests are the same. They possess a variety of personalities and temperaments, gifts and talents.

Without diminishing at all the special nature of the priestly call and office, we have to be patient when our priests don't live up to our personal expectations. If a priest fails or offends you, try to forgive him. We need to recognize, as St. Paul did 2000 years ago, that servants of the Lord are "earthen vessels." (Cf. II Cor 4:7)

The second point is that by Catholic law and theology priests are the leaders of the parish community. The *Code of Canon Law* says that: "The pastor is the proper shepherd of the parish entrusted to him, exercising pastoral care in the community entrusted to him under the authority of the Diocesan Bishop in whose ministry he has been called to share . . . He carries out for his community the duties of teaching, sanctifying, and governing." (Canon 519)

Clearly, the pastor has the duty to form a community that is one, holy, catholic and apostolic; to instill a Catholic vision in full conformity with the Universal Church. In exercising his authority, however, the pastor works most effectively when he listens to his people, when he engages them in a careful process of dialogue. He's not alone in his work, and it's important that he gathers a parish staff and volunteers who will share his vision and work closely with him for the good of the Church.

So to return to the question at the beginning of this article, "Are you willing to sacrifice an entire parish for the sake of one incompetent, uncaring priest?" The answer of course is no, but it's wrong to assume that your priest is incompetent and uncaring. Perhaps he doesn't possess a cheerful personality and ruffles parochial feathers on a weekly basis. Maybe his vision of the Church and style of management clash with yours. And perhaps he makes changes in the programs, practices, and schedules to which you've grown accustomed. But that's a little different from saying he's incompetent and uncaring.

The unity of the Church is a precious gift for which Jesus lived and died. Therefore, it's always my prayer that priest and people will work together in the name of Christ and for the good of His Church. I hope that the faithful will respect, support, and pray for their priests. And I expect priests to listen carefully to their people, to speak to them gently, and to care for them with love.

God promised His people, "I will give you shepherds after my own heart." (Jer 3:15) The Church does its very best to carry on the work of Jesus the Good Shepherd, by training, ordaining, and sending effective and compassionate priests. But keep in mind, short of Jesus Himself, there's no such thing as a perfect shepherd.

CHAPTER 38

When Preachers Fall from Grace

A recent headline in a Catholic website caught my attention: "Trust evaporating – Poll finds clergy trustworthiness slips precipitously." The poll surveyed attitudes about the clergy in Canada. According to the survey, 61 percent of Canadians trust church representatives, far below the 97 percent who trust firefighters and the 94 percent who trust nurses. The good news in this poll, if there is any, is that clergy still rank above the pollsters themselves (59 percent), journalists (48 percent), and politicians (just 15 percent). Small comfort it seems.

Although this particular story doesn't report it, without a doubt, the trustworthiness of clergy in the United States has suffered a similar sharp decline in recent years.

Most of this, of course, is related to the well-documented clergy sexual abuse crisis. And while Catholic priests have received most of the attention, there have been abuses and scandals in just about every church and denomination – evangelicals, mainline Protestants, Jewish, Muslim, and homemade religions to be sure.

The failure of clergy to live up to their calling is sad, but not new. One historian observes, "If polls could have been taken during the Reformation in the 15th and 16th centuries, or during the 18th century in Western Europe, the clergy might have ranked lower in the trust scale than they do now."

But my question is this: Does misbehavior of the messengers invalidate the truth of their message? And should it?

When I was in the minor seminary, we had very strict rules about the care of our dormitory rooms. They had to be neat and clean all the time – beds made, clothes in closets, windows spotless, sinks shining, and floors dust free. We were subject to room check at any time and a messy room could result in a couple of dreaded demerits.

The priest prefect on our corridor was a holy terror, especially demanding of clean rooms. But, we learned quickly, his personal faculty suite was a pigsty, a total disaster. When we objected that his messy room invalidated his strict enforcement of the law in our rooms, he said without apology, "Gentleman, even the lawbreaking judge must uphold the law."

And that, it seems to me, is how we have to approach the reality of imperfect preachers. Every preacher is a weak, flawed, sinful creature, "an earthen vessel" in Pauline terminology. But if we wait for perfect preachers our pulpits will be empty. Nonetheless, the truth of their message stands or falls on its own merits.

In more philosophical terms, the validity of the message comes from its inherent truth, not the personal worthiness of the messenger.

Catholic theology has an analogous situation, when we speak about "ex opere operato" in the dispensation of the sacraments. That means that the grace of the sacrament comes from the work itself, not from the sanctity of the minister. Even a priest in mortal sin can validly confer Baptism, forgive sins, and celebrate the Holy Sacrifice of the Mass.

So too, an unworthy preacher can deliver a truthful message. I'm conscious of this in my own ministry all the time. When I speak about abortion, stem cell research, gay marriage, immigration, or any other public issue, I make no claim to personal sanctity or moral superiority. I could be (and in fact am) an abject sinner but the message I present is valid because it's rooted in the Gospel of Christ and the teachings of the Church, realities strong enough to overcome my personal peccability.

An angry caller to a radio talk show I was on a few weeks ago challenged me on this precise point. "You're a hypocrite" he fairly shouted. If he was expecting a fight he was disappointed. "You're probably right," I agreed. "I think there's some hypocrisy in all of us whenever we fall short of what we want to be."

Objective truth has staying power. That's why Pope John Paul could speak of the *Splendor of the Truth* in his magnificent encyclical. Truth is a splendid reality that endures despite human sinfulness. "No darkness of error or sin can totally take away from man the light of God the Creator. In the depths of his heart there always remains a yearning for absolute truth and a thirst to obtain full knowledge of it," the Pope wrote.

People in walks of life other than clergy know the importance of teaching regardless of their personal short-comings. Parents are far from perfect yet they try to give good example to their children. Police officers aren't always award-winning citizens yet they have to arrest others. And, as our seminary prefect reminded us, even a lawbreaking judge must uphold the law.

This apparent dichotomy shouldn't be construed as a submission to moral complacency or an acceptance of personal hypocrisy. If we *deliberately* say one thing and do another, that's hypocrisy. But it's not hypocrisy to do our work and fulfill our obligations though we're scarred by personal imperfection.

So, when you read or hear about the moral failures of the clergy, in any denomination, you have every right to be disappointed. When they fail, pray for them, encourage them, and demand that they do better. But don't use their sins as an excuse to walk away from the Church or deny the truth of their message. When you do that, their failure becomes your problem.

CHAPTER 39

Reasons or Excuses?

You probably remember the parable Jesus told about the man who prepared a great feast for his family, friends, and neighbors. When all was ready he sent his servants to gather the invited guests. They refused to come, however, each offering an excuse: one had to check-out a new field he had purchased; another had to test-drive some new oxen; a third had just married and wanted to stay home with his bride. The master of the house then ordered other strangers to be invited so that his house would be filled and the banquet not wasted. (Cf. Lk 14:15-24)

I thought of that parable recently when I came across a newspaper article that described the religious practices of older Americans, those 45 and above. More specifically, the article explored why people lose their faith and, presumably, quit their churches.

Of the people polled, 58 percent said they lost their faith because of the hypocrisy of other worshippers and 57 percent pointed to the misbehavior of religious leaders. Some 39 percent said they quit because their church placed too much emphasis on money and 18 percent said there were too many rules.

Now I suppose that there's some validity in the reasons offered by the dropouts. After all, it is possible to be scandalized by the inappropriate behavior of church leaders or members of the congregation, and too much emphasis on money and rules can deflate any community.

But notice that the reasons given by those who lost their faith focus on the behavior of others without any commitment to self-examination. I'm reminded of the words of Jesus: "Stop judging that you may not be judged . . . Why do you notice the splinter in your brother's eye, but do not perceive the wooden beam in your own eye?" (Mt 7:1,3)

The people who have abandoned their faith are like those in the parable who refused to attend the banquet. But do they have legitimate reasons or self-serving excuses? And is it possible that people quit their churches for "reasons" other than those in the newspaper survey?

For starters, how about laziness? I suspect that some people abandon their faith simply because they don't have the energy to attend services on Sunday morning or participate in other programs offered by their churches. It's much more comfortable to stay home, lounge in bed, drink coffee, read the paper, and watch television, isn't it?

I'll bet that some people quit their churches because they have a guilty conscience. They're probably the same people who claim their churches have "too many rules." But is the problem "too many rules" or the fact that apathetic individuals don't like challenges posed by the teachings of Christ, some of which are very hard?

Some people lose their faith because they're in love with the world and the easy road it offers. Their lives are directed by the ungodly trio of materialism, hedonism, and atheism rather than the theological virtues of faith, hope, and love. They're professionals in their own secular endeavors but rank amateurs in the life of the spirit.

And, without a doubt, some people abandon their faith because God isn't very important to them. They attend church on Christmas and Easter but not at other times of the year. They see God as a safety net and turn to Him in times of national emergency or personal crisis, but rarely in other moments in their lives. Religious faith for them is a personal convenience rather than a fundamental commitment.

Laziness, a guilty conscience, secular values, and practical atheism – these aren't the convenient excuses people usually cite for losing their faith, but they are the real reasons, aren't they?

During our recent pilgrimage to Mexico, we visited a beautiful church that had an especially interesting pulpit. Among the ornate decorations of the formidable pulpit were several mirrors that ringed its circumference. Our tour guide mentioned that it's not unusual to see mirrors used that way in Mexican churches and explained that the purpose is to remind people that whenever they hear the Word of God they should be looking at themselves, not others.

That's not a bad habit for Christians to develop. If you tend to criticize the sins of your pastors and misbehavior of your neighbor, look into the mirror. If you find the demands of the Church or the teachings of Christ too challenging, look into the mirror. And if you've drifted away from God and find that He's no longer part of your life, look into the mirror.

Some in-depth mirror gazing will go a long way in purifying the Church and making it a more attractive home for others.

CHAPTER 40

The Need to Delete

If you look closely at your computer keyboard, you can tell which of the keys are used most often by the way they're worn. On my keyboard, the clear winner is the delete key. (For those blessed souls who have yet to travel to Computer Land, the delete key is used to erase something from your computer screen -a word, a sentence, a paragraph, or an entire story or article.   Just highlight what you want to erase, push the button and "poof," it's gone!)

The need to correct the written word certainly isn't new. In days gone by we used rubber erasers to correct an error. If it was written in pencil, it wasn't too bad, but ink presented a greater challenge. I'm sure I'm not the only one who scrubbed holes in notebook paper trying to eliminate a stubborn mistake. The use of typewriters for written work created a new wave of correction technology. First there was Wite-Out, that gooey stuff you'd smear over a mistake didn't really remove the error, just covered it. For a word or two, it was okay, but for more than that, it became pretty messy.

A major breakthrough came with the advent of correction tape. You remember that little piece of paper with a chalk like substance that was placed between the typewriter key and the written word. The idea was to lift-off the mistake and then retype the corrected version. The use of correction tape was clever but required enormous hand-eye coordination.

With electric typewriters came the automatic correction key. The correction ribbon now was built into the typewriter mechanism, and with just a few keystrokes, mistakes were easily eliminated.

Each of these correction systems had advantages and disadvantages, but none was very helpful in correcting carbon paper. (Readers over the age of 35, please explain to younger readers what carbon paper was and how it was used.)

But, back to my original point. As I look at my computer keyboard, it's clear that I make lots of mistakes. Without my delete button I'd be really lost and forced to live with my mistakes forever.

It's a little reflection of life itself.

We all make mistakes, have embarrassing moments, commit sins, and offend God and neighbor. But it's difficult to admit our faults, isn't it? During the presidential debates, George Bush was asked to name three mistakes he had made during his first term in office. He was unable, or unwilling, to do so. We don't do much better.

But recognizing our guilt is only the first step to renewal. We also have to forgive ourselves. Hey, after all, we're imperfect, flawed and limited human beings. We do the best we can but sometimes fall short of the mark. After we've admitted our sins and mistakes we need to hit the delete button and move on!

And what happens when people offend and betray us?

It's bound to happen someday. Maybe their slight was deliberate, maybe not. Maybe there was a reason, maybe not. Perhaps we don't understand it and we certainly don't like it. If we wish, we can brood over it forever.

But Christians don't have the luxury of brooding. Jesus demanded that His followers forgive one another. He taught us that our final judgment would be based on how we have forgiven others. And we pray everyday, "Forgive us our trespasses as we forgive those who trespass against us." In dealing with the sins of others, Christians need to hit the delete button and move on!

Our Lord Jesus, in His wisdom and love, has given us a delete button for the spiritual life. It's called the Sacrament of Penance. In this sacrament the powerful grace of God complements our frail human pursuit of forgiveness. Here we experience the remission of our sins so that we're not stuck in our guilt and shame forever; here we learn the art of self-forgiveness so that we can enjoy a new beginning; and here we are motivated to forgive others, released from the burden of sorrow and anger.

All of this presumes, of course, that we're sorry for our sins, are willing to make amends, and committed to doing better. The ability to forgive and be forgiven: it's a Christian requirement, an invitation, and a grace.

In short, we all have the need to delete. Unless, of course, you've never made a mistake.